C-1964

out of Print

MLN+

Happy Birthday to my sister Jill on her 10th birthday!

Love,
Tony
November, 1966

ABRAHAM LINCOLN

IN PEACE AND WAR

BY THE EDITORS OF
AMERICAN HERITAGE
The Magazine of History

AUTHOR
EARL SCHENCK MIERS

CONSULTANT
PAUL M. ANGLE
Secretary and Director, Chicago Historical Society

PUBLISHED BY
**AMERICAN HERITAGE
PUBLISHING CO., INC.**
New York

BOOK TRADE AND INSTITUTIONAL DISTRIBUTION BY
HARPER & ROW

FIRST EDITION
© 1964 by American Heritage Publishing Co., Inc., 551 Fifth Avenue, New York 17, New York. All rights reserved under Berne and Pan-American Copyright Conventions. Library of Congress Catalog Card Number: 64-22350. Trademark AMERICAN HERITAGE JUNIOR LIBRARY registered United States Patent Office.

In this patriotic print two great figures support the shield of the nation that "Washington made and Lincoln saved."

FOREWORD

Abraham Lincoln, a giant of a man in size and dignity, could not be overlooked; and he had a backwoods sense of humor that was not always easy to forgive. Even after he had led Union forces to victory in the Civil War, and had proclaimed freedom for the South's slaves, his staunch admirers were shocked and dismayed by his tendency to be reminded of a funny story amid the most desperate circumstances. When presented with a model of the experimental ship *Monitor* that might counter the South's ironclad threat *Merrimac*, he quipped: "All I can say is what the girl said when she put her foot in the stocking. 'It strikes me there's something in it.'"

Such humor, which often hid a grief on Lincoln's part that was too deep for words, was not in the fashion of the day. Just as some Americans of his own time had difficulty recognizing his greatness because of his human qualities, others in later generations failed to see him as anything but a storybook hero—reading by firelight in a log cabin, besting the bully Jack Armstrong, striking the shackles off the nation's slaves. It is a rare historian who has presented Lincoln as both the man of the frontier and the savior of his divided nation; both the teller of tall tales in his country store and the author of the Gettysburg Address; both the man of peace who joked his way out of a duel and the man of war who would not relent until the war was over.

Earl Schenck Miers has written such a combined portrait in the narrative of this book. He is assisted by a collection of Lincoln art that ranges from contemporary photographs to retrospective paintings, drawings, cartoons, and reconstructions. Neither warts nor jokes nor great decisions are spared, and as a result, young American readers may be enabled to meet the sixteenth President of the United States as he truly was, and as he has come to belong, in the words of Secretary of War Stanton, "to the ages."

—The Editors

Six new AMERICAN HERITAGE JUNIOR LIBRARY *books are published each year. Titles currently available are:*

ABRAHAM LINCOLN IN PEACE AND WAR
AIR WAR AGAINST HITLER'S GERMANY
IRONCLADS OF THE CIVIL WAR
THE ERIE CANAL
THE MANY WORLDS OF BENJAMIN FRANKLIN
COMMODORE PERRY IN JAPAN
THE BATTLE OF GETTYSBURG
ANDREW JACKSON, SOLDIER AND STATESMAN
ADVENTURES IN THE WILDERNESS
LEXINGTON, CONCORD AND BUNKER HILL
CLIPPER SHIPS AND CAPTAINS
D-DAY, THE INVASION OF EUROPE
WESTWARD ON THE OREGON TRAIL
THE FRENCH AND INDIAN WARS
GREAT DAYS OF THE CIRCUS
STEAMBOATS ON THE MISSISSIPPI
COWBOYS AND CATTLE COUNTRY
TEXAS AND THE WAR WITH MEXICO
THE PILGRIMS AND PLYMOUTH COLONY
THE CALIFORNIA GOLD RUSH
PIRATES OF THE SPANISH MAIN
TRAPPERS AND MOUNTAIN MEN
MEN OF SCIENCE AND INVENTION
NAVAL BATTLES AND HEROES
THOMAS JEFFERSON AND HIS WORLD
DISCOVERERS OF THE NEW WORLD
RAILROADS IN THE DAYS OF STEAM
INDIANS OF THE PLAINS
THE STORY OF YANKEE WHALING

American Heritage also publishes HORIZON CARAVEL BOOKS, *a similar series on world history, culture, and the arts. Titles currently available are:*

CORTES AND THE AZTEC CONQUEST
CAESAR
THE UNIVERSE OF GALILEO AND NEWTON
THE VIKINGS
MARCO POLO'S ADVENTURES IN CHINA
SHAKESPEARE'S ENGLAND
CAPTAIN COOK IN THE SOUTH PACIFIC
THE SEARCH FOR EARLY MAN
JOAN OF ARC
EXPLORATION OF AFRICA
NELSON AND THE AGE OF FIGHTING SAIL
ALEXANDER THE GREAT
RUSSIA UNDER THE CZARS
HEROES OF POLAR EXPLORATION
KNIGHTS OF THE CRUSADES

RIGHT: *A New Salem friend, seeing Abe in the shade with a book, asked what he was reading. Abe replied, "I'm not reading, I am studying law."*
LINCOLN NATIONAL LIFE FOUNDATION

COVER: *Before leaving Springfield, Illinois, on his long journey to Washington in 1860, Abraham Lincoln posed for this charcoal portrait.*
MEMORIAL HALL LIBRARY, ANDOVER, MASS.

FRONT ENDSHEET: *An 1890 lithograph sentimentally showed Lincoln revisiting his birthplace at Nolin Creek in Hardin County, Kentucky.*
LIBRARY OF CONGRESS

TITLE PAGE: *Soon after the fall of Fort Sumter, Commander-in-Chief Lincoln reviewed a regiment of Union volunteers at the White House.*
LIBRARY OF CONGRESS

BACK ENDSHEET: *Lincoln is hailed at City Point, Virginia, Grant's base for the final Union assault upon Richmond, the Confederate capital.*
CHICAGO HISTORICAL SOCIETY

CONTENTS

1	THE INDIANA FRONTIER	10
2	BOOKS AND POLITICS	24
3	MR. LINCOLN GOES TO WASHINGTON	44
4	THE GREAT DEBATE	56
5	RAILSPLITTER CANDIDATE	74
6	THE THREAT OF WAR	86
7	LINCOLN IS "WHIPPED AGAIN"	106
8	THE WAY TO VICTORY	122
9	WITH MALICE TOWARD NONE	136
	Acknowledgments	148
	For Further Reading	149
	Index	150

ILLUSTRATED WITH PAINTINGS, DRAWINGS, ENGRAVINGS, AND PHOTOGRAPHS OF THE PERIOD

1

THE INDIANA FRONTIER

Abe wondered if he would like his new mother. Standing between his older sister Sarah and their adopted cousin, Dennis Hanks, ten-year-old Abe watched the farm wagon creak up to the rough log cabin that the Lincolns called home. Something about the woman on the seat beside his pa instantly attracted Abe. She held her head high and proud. In her well-scrubbed face there was tenderness.

Tom Lincoln shouted at the horses to hide his embarrassment. When Tom had gone hunting a second wife back in Kentucky, he had talked big about his place in Little Pigeon Creek, Indiana. An old sweetheart, Sarah Bush Johnston, a widow, had believed him—at least to the point of marrying Tom and coming to Little Pigeon Creek with her own three youngsters and household belongings.

What she saw, looking down from the wagon seat, told her that Tom Lincoln had stretched the truth. The cabin which had been crude to begin with, was now run-down and sagging. But with an affectionate swat, she hustled her own John, Sarah, and Matilda down from the wagon. She had made her bargain and would live with it.

Abe was fascinated by the contents of the wagon. There was a table, a set of chairs, a large clothes chest, cooking utensils, knives, forks, and bedding. There was a bureau that his pa whispered was worth forty dollars—a piece of furniture that outshone anything in Little Pigeon Creek. Tom Lincoln, a practical man who thought the bureau was too good for them, wanted to turn it into cash.

There his new wife balked. Changes were coming into the Lincoln household—of that fact Tom Lincoln need never have a moment's doubt—but selling the bureau was not one of

The cabin in this photograph was reconstructed on the site of the first home Abe Lincoln could remember—at Knob Creek, Kentucky. As Abe grew he learned to wield an axe to split rails for zigzag fences like these.

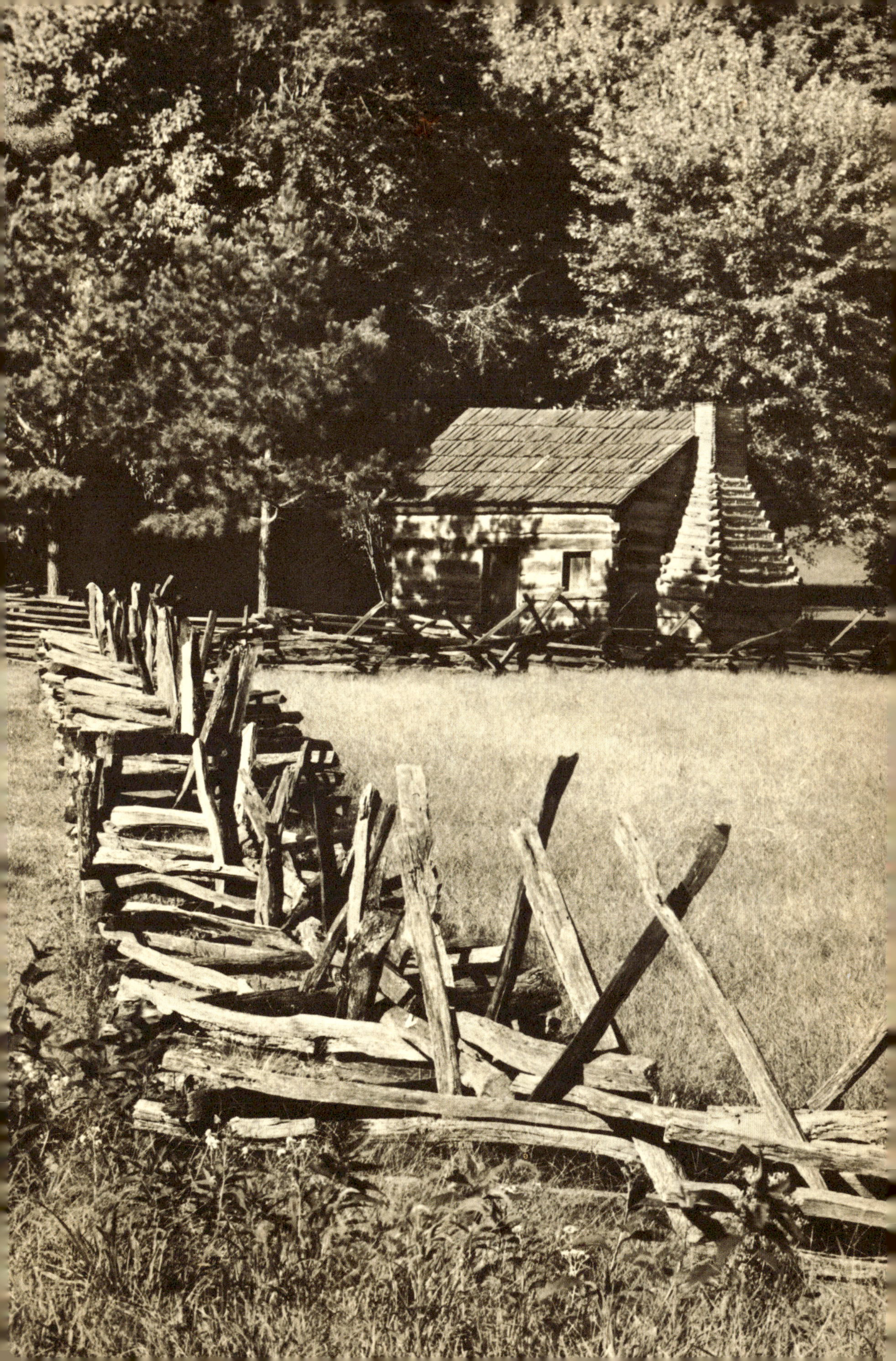

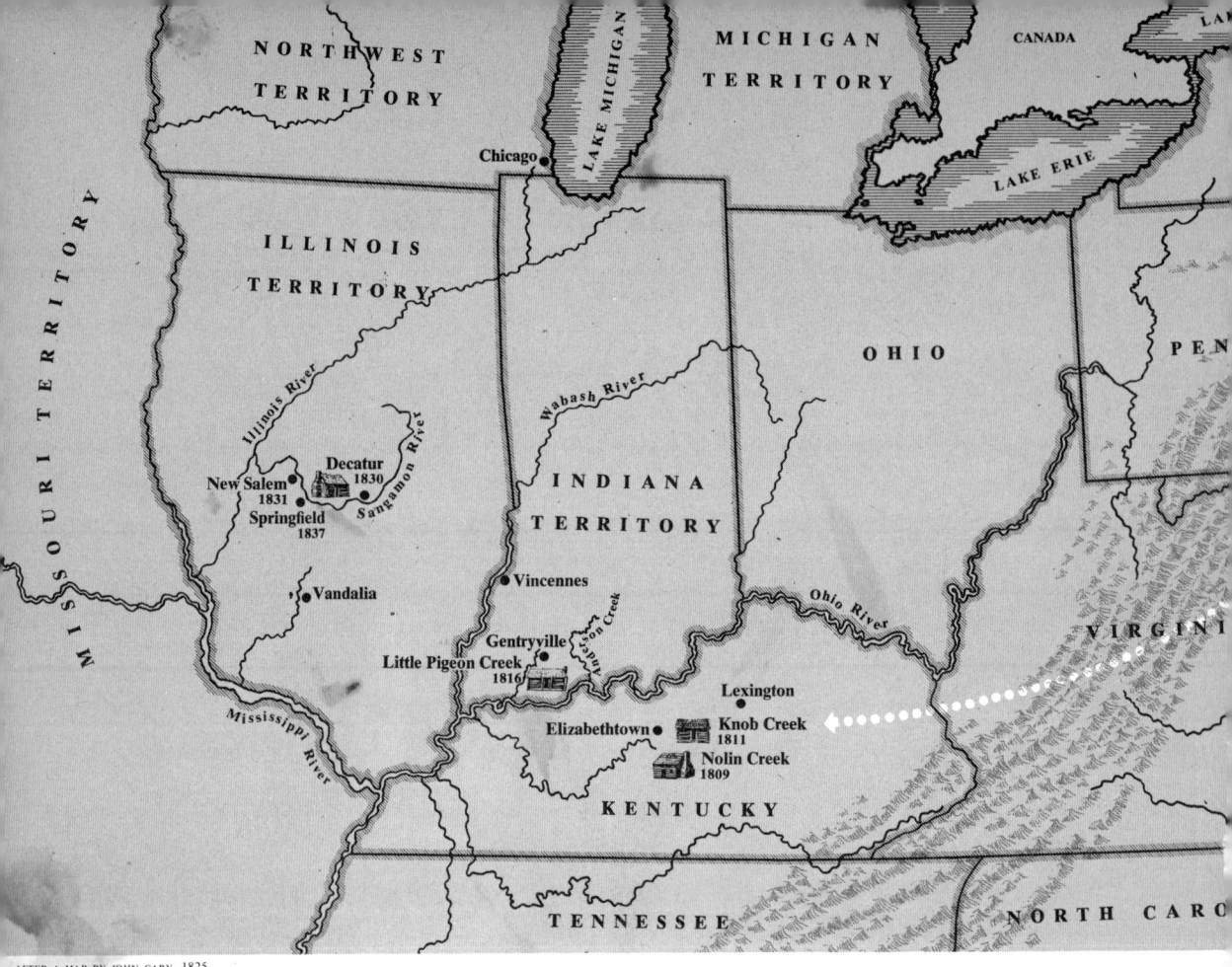

them. Instead, Tom set to work repairing the cabin as best he could. From dawn till bedtime Abe's stepmother was a whirlwind of energy and good sense. Neatness was her passion.

Washed until he glowed and tucked in a warm, clean bed, Abe must have thought back over the years before his stepmother came. Of his early childhood in Kentucky he remembered little. The family Bible told him that he had been born February 12, 1809, in a backwoods cabin three miles south of Hodgenville. His own first recollection was of the place on Knob Creek where the Lincolns later moved.

Abe knew nothing about his family any further back than his grandfather. That Lincoln, also named Abraham, had brought his family from Virginia to Kentucky around 1782 and had settled about twenty miles east of Louisville. Young Abe had a kind of horrified fascination for the fact that his namesake had been killed from ambush by a skulking Indian. Modern historians, however, have managed to trace the family of Abraham Lincoln to Samuel Lincoln, a weaver's apprentice, who settled in Hingham, Massachusetts, in 1637. Subsequently the Lincoln clan, always industrious and respectable, wandered down through Pennsylvania and New Jersey

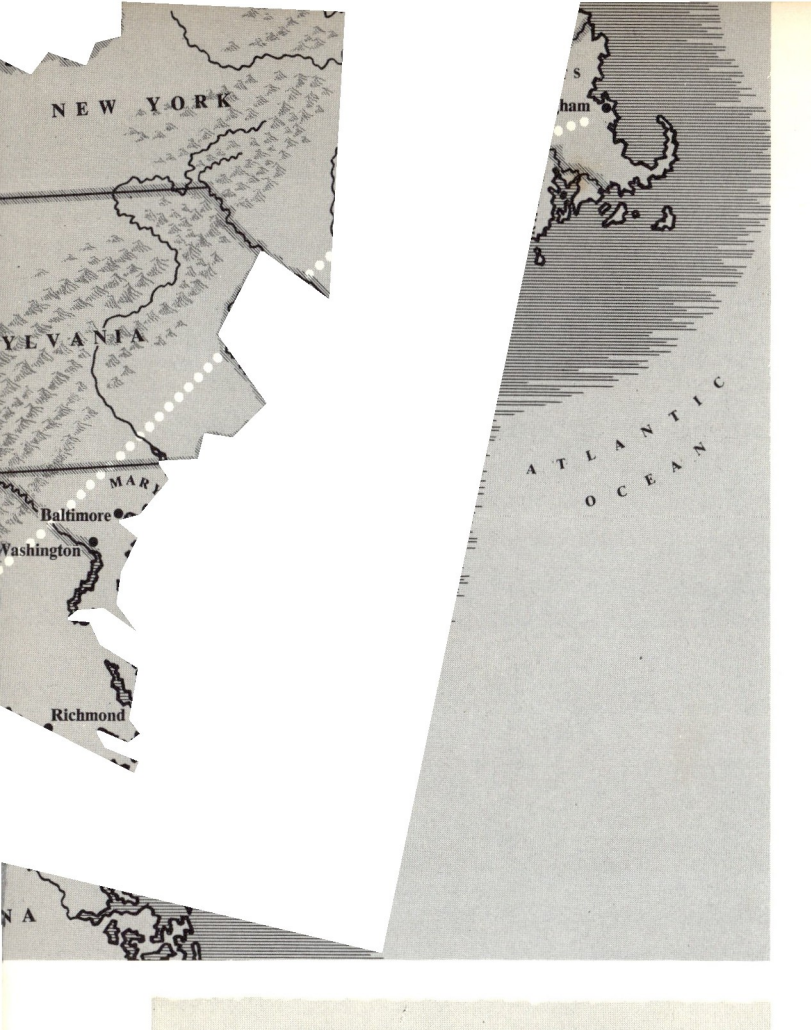

THE LINCOLNS' ROUTE WEST

On the first page of a thumbnail autobiography drafted in 1859 (left), Lincoln confessed that he sprang from "undistinguished families—second families, perhaps I should say." The westward route that his ancestors are thought to have taken from Hingham, Massachusetts, through Virginia to Elizabethtown, Kentucky, can be traced on this copy of an 1825 map of the United States. (Notice the misplacement of Lake Michigan.) The cabins superimposed on the map mark locations to which the restless Tom Lincoln moved his family.

In this painting of a pioneer family on the move, the father leads oxen on the trail west, while the mother rides in the wagon with the youngest children and her household goods.

before they settled down in Virginia.

Although Abe's father may have told his future second wife some fancy stories about Little Pigeon Creek, Tom Lincoln was in other respects a reliable, hard-working man. By the time he settled in Knob Creek, he had become a landholder of moderate means who had often been called for jury duty, had once served as an appraiser of an estate, and had acted as a supervisor of roads. True, he could not read and his writing skill extended only to the painful scrawling of his name, but neighbors clearly trusted him for his enterprise and his thrift.

Little is known of Abe's mother, Nancy Hanks Lincoln. Apparently she was born February 5, 1784, and married Tom Lincoln when she was twenty-two. She signed her name with a mark. Friends remembered that she was kind, intelligent, and deeply religious.

For a time the couple lived in Elizabethtown, Kentucky, where Tom worked as a carpenter, and here their first child, Sarah, was born on February 10, 1807. Although Tom owned a farm on Mill Creek (purchased before his marriage) and two town lots in Elizabethtown, he decided the following December to buy a second farm on Nolin Creek, eighteen miles southeast of Elizabethtown. There Abe was born.

From his birthplace, Abe and his family moved to Knob Creek in 1811. Close by their new cabin passed the old Wilderness Trail from Louisville to Nashville. From their door the Lincolns could watch pioneers moving west in lumbering covered wagons followed by cattle kicking up great clouds of dust. There were also peddlers who came hawking clocks, pots, pins, and combs. Preachers rode past, and sometimes an overseer or slave dealer appeared with Negroes in chains. Baptists like the Lincolns, were bitterly opposed to slavery, and were likely to turn grimly away at such moments. Down the road two miles stood a log schoolhouse, run first by Zachariah Riney and later by Caleb Hazel. There, at sporadic intervals, Abe and Sarah received rudimentary instruction in the three R's.

There were sad times for the Lincolns in Knob Creek. A third child, Thomas, died in infancy. Then Tom Lincoln's ownership of his farms came into question, for land titles were vaguely worded in those days and hard to substantiate. When he had to sell his Mill Creek farm in 1814, Tom discovered that thirty-eight acres of the land did not belong to him, and he lost money he had been counting on. Next he was drawn into the courts over a faulty title on the Nolin Creek farm.

When a claim was filed accusing him of squatting on the Knob Creek place, his eyes turned northward to Indiana where government surveys guaranteed proper titles. In December of 1816 Tom mounted his family on horseback and they struck off into the wilderness. And wilderness it was. An early settler described the Indiana Territory as nothing but "woods, woods, woods, as far as the world extends!"

The Lincolns arrived in what is now Spencer County in late winter. For several bitterly cold weeks Tom Lincoln was forced to house his family in a three-sided shelter of logs roofed over with branches. The only way they could keep warm was to feed a roaring fire on the open side both day and night. For water, Abe was obliged to

The only photograph of Sarah Bush Lincoln shows her close to the end of her hard, frontier life.

15

trudge back and forth to a spring a mile away at least once a day.

When spring showed signs of breaking through the savage winter, Tom Lincoln and Abe got busy chopping down trees and building their new cabin. Soon the air was filled with the scent of wild crab apple blossoms, and it was time to clear fields for the spring planting. Building and clearing —all work that had to be done with an axe. In later years Abe recalled that from this time until he was twenty-three he "was almost constantly handling that useful implement."

One day Abe heard a flutter of wings while he was in the cabin. He grabbed his rifle, sighted through a crack in the log wall, and killed a wild turkey. But as he watched the bird plummet earthward, something sickened within him. He realized then that it was wrong to kill. "Never since," Abe Lincoln later wrote of that day, "[has he] pulled a trigger on any larger game."

As Abe grew in size and muscle, he also gained in sensitivity and good humor. He was glad when Thomas and Elizabeth Sparrow, who had been his mother's childhood guardians, moved up from Kentucky bringing with them Dennis Hanks, his cousin,

The rough beauty of life in Indiana was painted by the Swiss watercolorist Carl Bodmer when he visited the territory in 1833. Notable features in this view of a cabin yard in which a woman is hanging out wash are the open loft, the spring house (foreground), the split-rail fence, and the omnipresent stumps.

17

who was then nineteen. Nine-year-old Abe thrived on Dennis' company and friendship, and they soon became inseparable.

But tragedy had followed the Lincolns to Indiana. In September of 1818 an outbreak of an illness known as the milksick struck at Spencer County. Now doctors believe that the milksick, then one of the most dread afflictions of the wilderness, is caused by drinking the milk of cows who have browsed on poisonous white snakeroot or rayless goldenrod. All that was known of the disease in 1818 was how it affected a victim. A white coating appeared on the tongue, and there was a burning sensation within the vital organs; then the tongue turned a brownish color while the patient's hands and feet grew colder and his pulse beat more slowly.

In that superstitious time, when no sensible farmer would plant a crop until the position of the moon was exactly right, it seemed as though one watched Death himself walk into a cabin and take hold of his victim. The whole neighborhood shuddered when Betsy and Tom Sparrow contracted the milksick and died within a few days. Tom Lincoln, still a good carpenter, made coffins for his old friends.

In October Nancy Hanks Lincoln came down with the same illness. Tom, Abe, Sarah, and Dennis stood by helplessly, watching her die. Tom sadly nailed together another coffin. There was not a minister within miles, so Tom Lincoln, pioneer father and husband, stood by his children as he preached the service and laid his beloved wife Nancy to rest beside the Sparrows.

No one had much to say afterward. They walked back to the cabin through the radiant autumn sunshine and picked up the loose ends of their lives. Tom, with the help of Dennis and Abe, tried to make the farm support them all, but the crops were poor and scanty. Sarah did the cooking, and

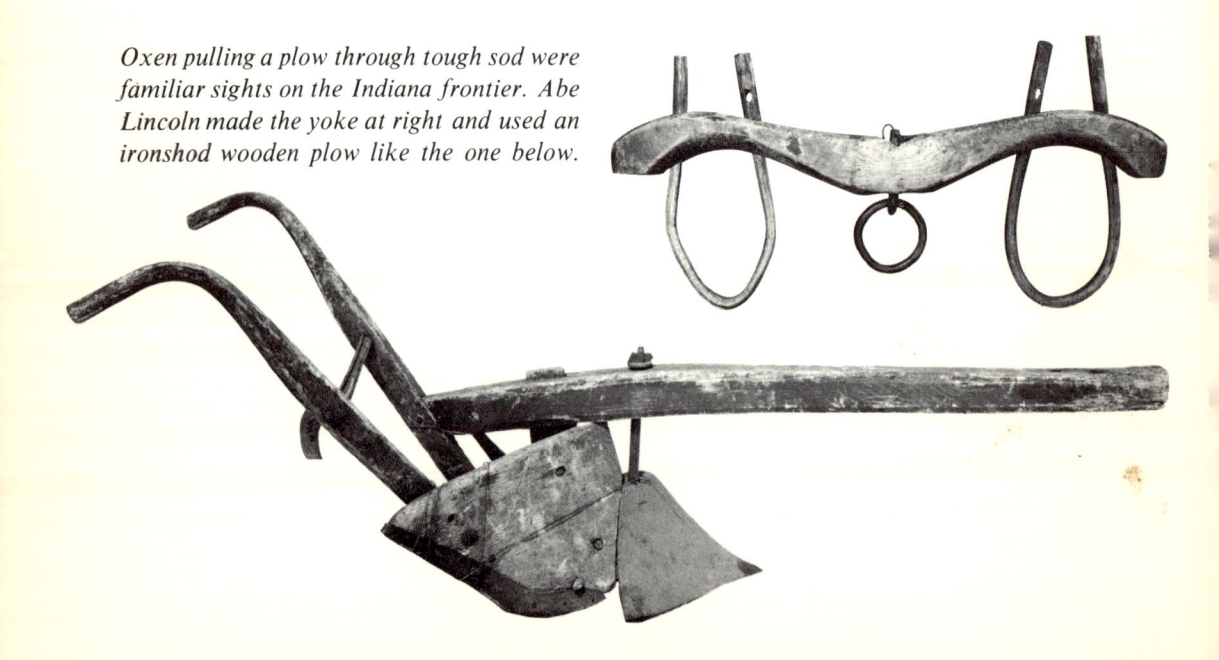

Oxen pulling a plow through tough sod were familiar sights on the Indiana frontier. Abe Lincoln made the yoke at right and used an ironshod wooden plow like the one below.

Not all the timber Abe chopped and split was used for fence rails; he also earned money by supplying fuel for wood-burning river steamers like this one sketched by Basil Hall in 1829.

attempted to keep up with the cleaning, mending, and washing. But she was only twelve when her mother died, and not strong enough to handle such hard work alone. Tom watched his brood losing their battle with the crops, and the dirt, and the flies, and knew he must find a new wife and mother for the Lincolns.

So, in the early winter of 1819, he hitched up a horse and rode back to Elizabethtown, Kentucky, to court Sarah Bush Johnston. Sally, as she was called, accepted his proposal and married Tom Lincoln on December 2. An energetic, optimistic woman, she quickly recovered from the shock of seeing the tumbledown cabin and the ragged children, caught her breath, and set to work.

Most of all Sally worked on Abe. It had not taken her long to see that Abe had a quick mind, full of promise, and she was determined to make him outshine Little Pigeon Creek like her forty-dollar bureau. Abe loved his stepmother—in later years he called her his "angel of a mother"—and was determined to do his best for her. She wanted him back in school, when Tom could spare him, and back to school he went under teachers named Andrew Crawford, a man known as Sweeney, and Azel W. Dorsey.

Abe walked to and from school on a trail that wound along for a mile and a quarter. When he entered the one-room schoolhouse he saw pupils ranging from small children to big, husky farm boys. And the din they were making was incredible. This was one of the famous "blab" schools of the era. To make certain that all his other charges were studying while he taught one grade, the schoolmaster had them recite their lessons out loud,

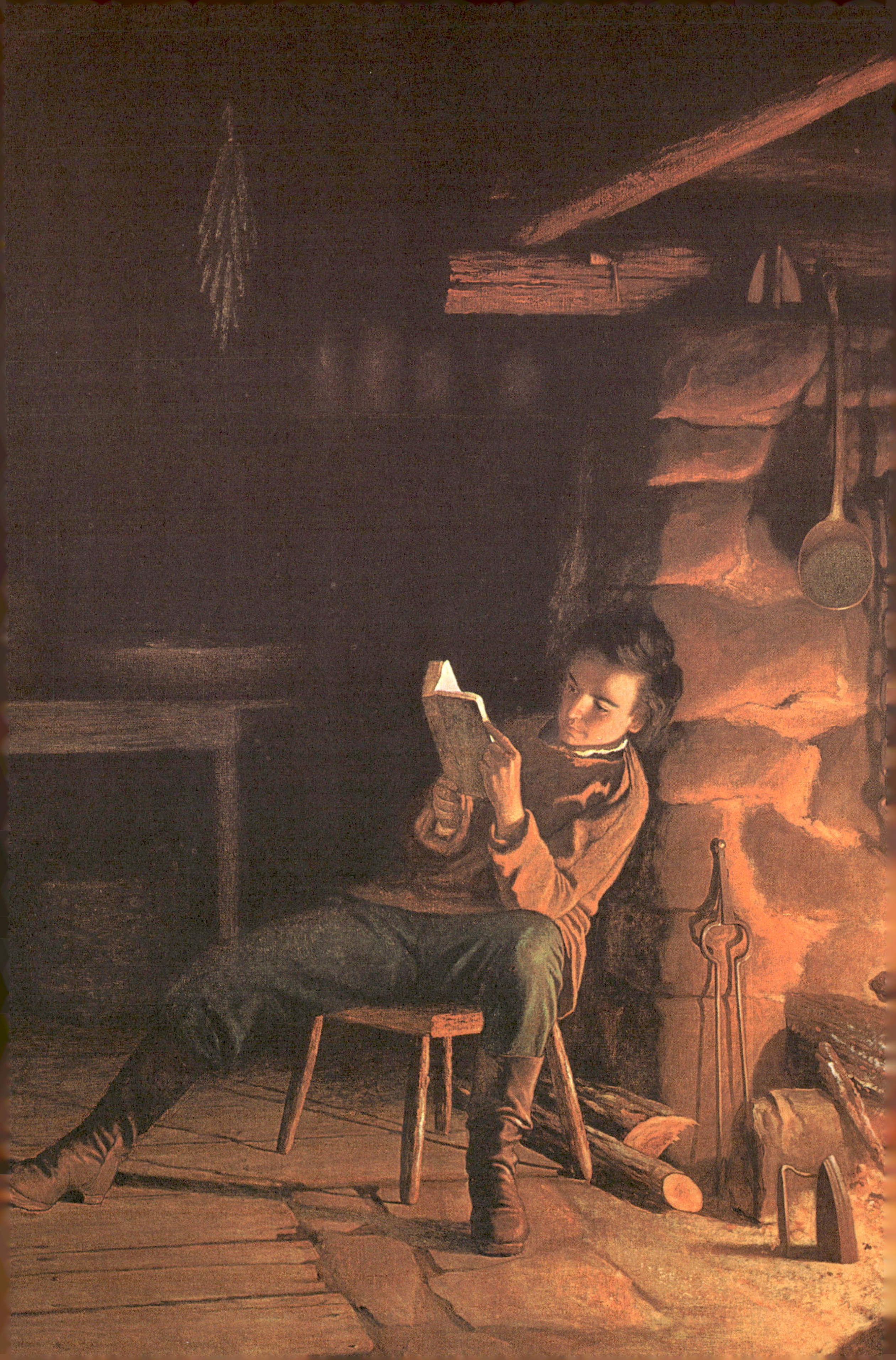

over and over. Abe's formal education, he recalled one day, lasted not more than a year. At the age of twenty-one he "did not know much," though he "could read, write, and cipher to the Rule of Three," which was about as well as anyone (including the schoolmasters) could do in the Indiana of that period.

But Abe enjoyed books and became a good reader. He read and reread *Robinson Crusoe*, *Pilgrim's Progress*, *Aesop's Fables*, and Grimshaw's *History of the United States*. Books were his constant companions—when he plowed a field and reached the end of a furrow he would pull out a volume and mull over a page or two while giving his horse a few minutes' rest.

Devoted as Sally Lincoln was to Abe, she must have seen that he was an easygoing sort of young man. He farmed out of a sense of duty, and often hired out to neighbors who seldom paid him more than a boy's wages of twenty-five cents a day. A feeling of unworthiness may have led him to write the lines of doggerel preserved as the earliest specimen of his handwriting:

"Abraham Lincoln, his hand and pen, He will be good but God knows when."

The world of Little Pigeon Creek, Indiana, was as rough-hewn as a log cabin—a world of the hard toil of driving plows through knotty sod, of heavy whiskey drinkers, of believers in charms and witches, of raw humor and practical jokes; of quilting bees, and house raisings, and square dances now and then; of homemade clothes and hard-to-come-by money, of barefoot women and children, and of dirt everywhere.

Abe was always a sociable youngster. He could tell a story easier than Tom Lincoln could scrawl his name. Whenever he went down to Gentryville, a mile and a half from the Lincolns' cabin, he would keep the crowd in the village store laughing by the hour. Dennis often accompanied Abe and enjoyed listening to his tales. But

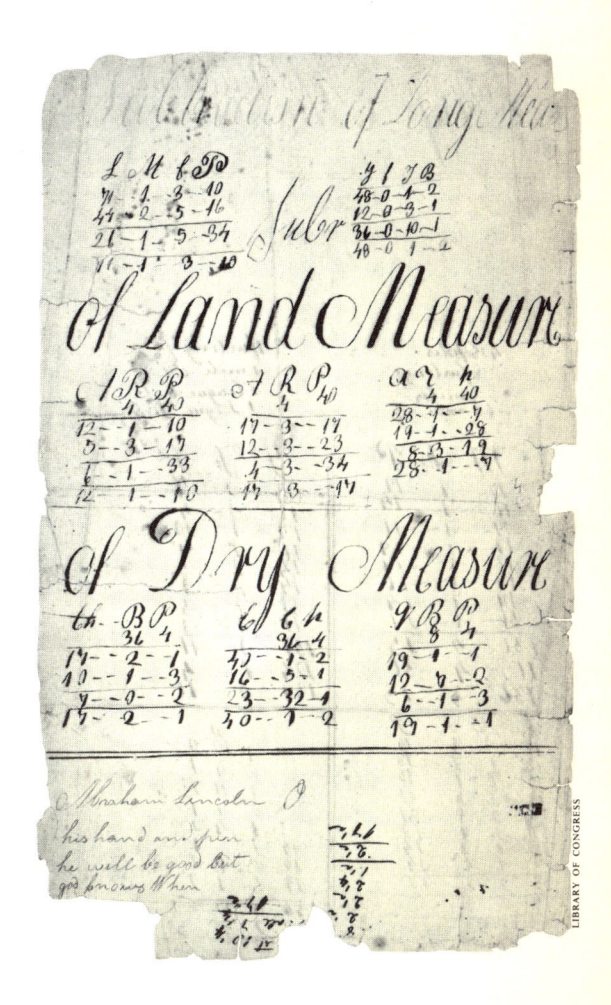

One of the best-known paintings of Lincoln's boyhood is the firelit scene at left by Eastman Johnson. Besides reading, Abe learned arithmetic by copying sums and measures into his notebook (right). The verse was probably not his own invention.

when the hour neared midnight, his sleepiness would get the better of his good temper. Dennis would then try cussing Abe out to see if he could get his cousin started out of the store and on the way home. But Abe loved a crowd and would keep talking as long as there was anyone to listen.

Life was not just reading and telling stories. Abe went looking for work when he was seventeen and once made a sizeable piece of money, a fact that stuck in his memory like the wild turkey he had shot and killed. About sixteen miles from where the Lincolns lived flowed Anderson Creek, which with an occasional twist through high bluffs, finally managed to reach the Ohio. Where the creek and river met stood the prosperous town of Troy—a good anchoring place for river steamers. Abe found a man-sized job there helping the ferry keeper.

In the rare moments when he had some time off, Abe busied himself building a small scow. One day, because of this craft, luck played into his hands. Two passengers wanted to reach a steamer in a hurry and Abe's scow was the only means available. So he rowed, sweating for dear life, made the steamer, landed his passengers, and threw their carpetbags on board. In return, they each flipped down a silver half dollar. Abe shook his head, finding it a revelation that "I, a poor boy, had earned a dollar in less than a day."

An even greater adventure on the river lay ahead. The richest man in Gentryville was James Gentry. He had managed to acquire more than a thousand acres of Indiana land, and establish a trading post around which the village named after him was situated.

Gentry's son Allen was one of Abe's best friends. Knowing his father had produce and other cargo to move to market in New Orleans, Allen persuaded Gentry to consign a load to Abe and himself. Excitedly the two boys began to build themselves a crude but sturdy flatboat. In late December of 1828, when Abe was nineteen, they loaded their cargo onto the completed boat and set off. The boys floated down the Ohio and into the Mississippi which would take them to the bustling port of New Orleans.

It was a great trip for Abe who acted as bow hand and "was paid eight dollars per month from the time of starting to his returning home." Most of the voyage was pleasant and uneventful. However, at a place described as "the plantation of a Madame Duchesne, not far from New Orleans," a band of Negro brigands armed with hickory clubs attacked the craft. The watchful crew fought desperately to save their cargo. Both parties were bleeding when the battle ended, but Abe and Allen had managed to beat off their marauders. Then they "hastily swung into the stream and floated down the river till daylight." The boys docked in New Orleans with their cargo intact.

Abe was in a world now that neither

Kentucky nor Indiana could ever equal. He strolled the narrow, cobblestone streets of the exciting, sophisticated city seeing its old, foreign-style houses with their fanciful iron railings, and hearing the sounds of a metropolis unlike any other in America.

He heard people speaking French, Spanish, and Portuguese. He saw trees bedecked with funereal streamers of Spanish moss. He saw the great levee where bales of cotton and hogsheads of sugar and tobacco were piled high ready for shipping. Along the levee he saw mile-long lines of flatboats and river steamers waiting to transfer their cargoes to the three-masters of the foreign trade. He saw the city's famed slave market where men, women, and children were sold at auction. He was, he knew, a very long way from Little Pigeon Creek, Indiana.

After selling their cargo and sightseeing for a while, the boys returned home. Abe slipped back into his old life of reading, farming, and being an obedient son.

A flatboat that has come down the Mississippi is towed past the busy New Orleans waterfront in this 1840 aquatint. In the foreground a levee is being repaired by Negroes such as those Abe saw in the slave market.

2

BOOKS AND POLITICS

Abe earned twenty-four dollars from his trip to New Orleans. According to the custom of the time, he gave this sum to his father.

But twenty-four dollars was not enough to improve the fortunes of the Lincoln family. For two years after Abe's return to Indiana crops were poor and money scarce. To add to their discontent, letters from John Hanks, Abe's cousin, extolled the vast richness of the land in central Illinois where he had settled. Early in 1830 when the milksick broke out in Indiana too, Tom Lincoln decided that he had seen enough of trouble. Family and possessions were loaded onto a farm wagon, and on March 1 the Lincolns started for Illinois.

Abe, just come of age, urged forward a team of oxen. After four or five days the party came to Vincennes, splashed across the Wabash, and eventually arrived in Decatur, Illinois, where a dozen or so rough log cabins faced onto the muddy town square.

At a point on the Sangamon River ten miles southwest of Decatur, where the forest ended and the prairie rolled on, the Lincolns started life anew. Ten acres of land were cleared and fenced. Big, willing, rawboned Abe, an axe always in his hand, became the best rail splitter in the neighborhood.

Yet misery seemed to follow the Lincolns wherever they went. Ague and fever, the common lot of Illinois pioneers, weakened the family on the Sangamon. Then a hard winter set in with blizzards and below-freezing temperatures. Cows and horses, floundering in the deep snow, were devoured by starving wolf packs. Hoping to change the family's luck, Abe, his stepbrother John Johnston, and his cousin John Hanks planned another trip to New Orleans. The first floods of spring found them paddling a large canoe down the Sangamon.

They beached the canoe at a ferry landing near Springfield and walked into town to look for Denton Offut. A

INDIANA TERRITORY STATE MEMORIAL, VINCENNES UNIVERSITY

Lincoln first saw a printing press when his family passed through Vincennes, Indiana. This painting shows Abe with Elihu Stout, frontier newspaperman and owner of the press.

Sturdy craft, like the flatboat being constructed in the drawing above, were used to freight goods down-river to Southern ports. Below, New Salem villagers watch as Abe and his crew try to get their flatboat off the dam on the Sangamon River.

good merchant but an unreliable friend, Offut had promised to supply them a cargo. After searching through most of the taverns in town, they finally found him. Offut, a prodigious drinker and extravagant talker, admitted sheepishly that he had forgotten they would also need a boat. Undaunted, the three boys agreed to build a flatboat for wages of twelve dollars each a month. They finished the craft in a month and loaded it with corn, barreled pork, and live pigs.

Downstream, at the mill dam at the hamlet of New Salem, the flatboat struck the lip of the dam, rode over it part way, and hung there, its stern slowly filling with water. Villagers guffawed, offering advice. Unflustered, Abe ordered part of the cargo unloaded, let the water out of the overhanging bow with a borrowed augur, then plugged up the hole. Admiring villagers watched the boat pass over the dam.

The remainder of the trip was somewhat less hazardous although there were always sand bars, tricky currents, and unexpected storms to contend with. This time Abe remained in New Orleans for nearly a month. Then he worked his way back shoveling coal on a Mississippi steamer. By the time he reached home, in July of 1831, he had decided to strike out on his own. After telling his family about his adventures, Abe announced his plans, and set off for New Salem.

The little town on a bluff of the Sangamon was scarcely more than a settlement hidden in a prairie cornfield. Here, an early inhabitant declared, "the fittest survived and the rest the Lord seen fittin' to take away." But Abe was as roughhewn as the settlement. For fifteen dollars a month he worked in a store which Denton Offut had just opened in New Salem, and slept in the back room. He was soon known for miles around as the best storyteller in the whole countryside.

Abe's growing popularity upset a local gang of roughnecks known as "the Clary's Grove Boys." These wild-looking young hellions respected brute strength and very little else. By their standards Offut's constant bragging about Abe's muscular prowess amounted to an out-and-out insult.

The leader of the Clary's Grovers was ox-like Jack Armstrong, who was forever pulling practical jokes, wrestling, and laying bets on cockfights and races. As boasts flew back and forth between the two factions it became inevitable that Abe and Jack would tangle. The prospect of such a fight delighted the whole community.

Finally a day was set, wagers were made, and the fight was on. Angered by Abe's ability to hold off his bear-hug tactics, Jack brought his boot heel down hard on his opponent's foot. The next thing Jack knew he had been lifted high in the air in a powerful grip and slammed down on the ground. Winded and amazed, he looked up at Abe, allowed that he had been "pawed" enough, and then made

When Abe settled in New Salem in 1831, his ready wit and lean strength gained him quick acceptance. When he beat Jack Armstrong, the local champ, in a wrestling match (above), he became the village favorite.

friends. Thereafter Abe never found more loyal supporters than the Clary's Grove Boys.

In March of 1832, when he was twenty-three, Abe Lincoln decided to follow the advice of some of his New Salem friends. He announced his candidacy for the Illinois legislature. Mentor Graham, the local schoolmaster who had been very kind to Abe, probably helped the young man draw up his political platform for publication in the Sangamo Journal.

In advocating the improvement of the Sangamon River, better educational facilities, and lower interest rates, Abe spoke for his New Salem neighbors. He was born, Abe wrote, "in the most humble walks of life," and if elected the voters "will have conferred a favor upon me, for which I shall be unremitting in my labors to compensate." Yet he was willing to accept defeat: "I have been too familiar with disappointments to be very much chagrined."

That April, before the balloting, there was an Indian scare. The Sac and Fox tribe, once the proud possessors of the rich farmland of northern Illinois, were dissatisfied with their allotted land west of the Mississippi. Under their war chief, Black Hawk, a party of braves recrossed the river and began a bloody campaign to reclaim their former home. A volunteer militia was hurriedly formed to put an end to the raiding and burning.

Abe signed up for duty with a company of thirty-day volunteers made up mostly of neighbors and Clary's Grove Boys. They soon elected him their captain—the most satisfying incident in his life, Abe said afterwards. Although he did not have much in the way of military polish, he made up for it with common sense. For instance when his men found a fence blocking their line of march, Abe ordered: "Halt. This company will break ranks . . . and form again on the other side of that gate."

After serving two more thirty-day stints as a private, Lincoln returned home two weeks before the election. He was running as a Whig, which is what the conservatives opposing the Democrats were then called. Although this was a handicap in a region dominated by the radical "whole-hog Jackson men" of the Democratic Party, he traveled the countryside in a cheerful mood. Often he seized a pitchfork and worked right along with any farmer who was willing to hear him out.

Dressed in an old straw hat and a calico shirt, Abe made a speech in Springfield on the last day of the election. He impressed a prominent Whig, Stephen T. Logan, who wrote: "He was a very tall, gawky, and rough-looking fellow then; his pantaloons didn't meet his shoes by six inches. But after he began speaking, I became very much interested in him." Logan remembered Abe after the election—which the young man never had a chance of winning. He ran eighth in a field of thirteen, but he did win 277 of the 300 votes cast in the New Salem precinct.

Faced with the necessity of holding skin and bone together, Abe thought of becoming a blacksmith, or a lawyer, but settled at last on a partnership in a general store with William F. Berry.

Black Hawk, who led a futile armed uprising against the settlers in Illinois, posed for his portrait wearing a medal won in the War of 1812.

NEW SALEM DAYS

At the entrance to the reconstructed village of New Salem stands a statue of the youthful Lincoln—in his hands the emblem of his frontier life, an axe, and the symbol of his new life, a book. Among the many restorations in the village are the Rutledge tavern (below), where Abe boarded, and the Lincoln-Berry store, where he discovered that he could never be a shopkeeper.

On March 6, 1833, the firm of Lincoln and Berry obtained a license "to keep tavern" in New Salem for one year. But trade was slow and Abe was pretty much a failure as a merchant of salt, thread, and firearms, or as a trader of muslin and calico for eggs and bacon. The business, Abe said, "did nothing but get deeper and deeper in debt"—a fact that should not have surprised Berry, who dipped a cup into the whiskey barrel at every opportunity. Lincoln hated drinking, complaining that liquor left him feeling "flabby and undone." But Berry consumed enough for both, and by January 10, 1835, had drunk himself into the grave. Liable for Berry's debts as well as his own, Abe called the $1,100 he now owed "the National Debt." It took years for him to pay off the full amount.

Still, Abe managed to eke out an existence. Things began to look up a bit when he received an appointment as postmaster of New Salem on May 7, 1833. Abe insisted that the appointment proved the office was "too insignificant to make my politics an objection." A neighbor wrote: "The Post Master (Mr. Lincoln) is very careless about leaving his office open and unlocked during the day—half the time I go in and get my papers, etc., without anyone being there." But Abe never made a journey without carrying inside his hat the letters belonging to the people in the neighborhood. Reading free the newspapers that came into the office, he benefited

31

politically from a growing knowledge of the affairs of the countryside.

Abe accepted any extra work that he was offered. He split rails. He worked at the mill. Serving as clerk at election time paid him a dollar, and returning the poll book to Springfield paid another two dollars and fifty cents. In late 1833 came the chance to serve as deputy to John Calhoun, the county surveyor. Borrowing books from Calhoun, and aided by schoolmaster Graham, Abe mastered surveying and mathematics. During the next three years—with a compass and chain and a horse that he procured on credit—he located several roads still in use, and surveyed the towns of Petersburg, Bath, New Boston, Albany, and Huron.

Abe grew wise to frontier manners, and frontier politics. In 1834, when he decided to run again for the Illinois legislature, he was suspicious of the support that an old but shrewd friend was giving him. The friend, a Democrat and the local justice of the peace, bore the unusual name of Bowling Green. Lincoln's suspicions were well-founded, for Green was encouraging

Lincoln lived in New Salem during its brief boom in 1833. This painting shows the village on the high bluff at left, and the mill and dam on the Sangamon River below. Between the cabins at far left is Jack Armstrong enjoying a favorite sport—rolling a friend down the bluff in a barrel.

him in order to take votes away from John Todd Stuart of Springfield, the county's Whig leader. But Stuart himself advised Abe to go along with the game, reasoning that votes for any Whig candidates were good votes. Meanwhile Stuart informed the Whigs of Green's plot. They in turn concentrated the campaign against the lone Democratic candidate. The Whigs swept to victory in the county with Abe Lincoln as their best vote-getter.

Stuart's fondness for Abe grew. A mild-mannered, well-educated man, Stuart sparked his young friend's serious study of law. He lent Abe books on the subject, and smiled to himself when he learned that Abe had used his own money to buy other books at auction.

Just before the state legislature was to convene in late November, 1834,

ATTENTION!
THE PEOPLE!!

A. LINCOLN, ESQ'R.,

OF *Sangamon County*, one of the *Electoral Candidates*, will ADDRESS the PEOPLE

This Evening!!

At Early Candlelighting, at the ☞ OLD COURT ROOM, ✍ (Riley's Building.) By request of
MANY CITIZENS.

Thursday, April 9th, 1840.

Abe borrowed some money from an old friend, invested in his first tailor-made suit of clothes, and caught the stage to the capital of Illinois. Life in Vandalia must have been exciting for the freshman legislator from Sangamon. Sharing a room with socially and politically prominent John Stuart opened a new world for Abe. He mingled with men and women whose discussions covered subjects as widely diversified as national and state politics, internal improvements, education, and judicial procedure. Lincoln matured and he learned.

He took his seat on the first floor of the rickety capitol building where the House of Representatives met. Occasionally a speaker would have to shout over the din of falling plaster. Long tables were provided as desks for the legislators, and they were most convenient for resting legs upon. In this, his first session, Abe played a minor role. As a freshman legislator, his assigment to the Committee on the Public Accounts and Expenditures was unassuming. But Stuart, forced through a heavy schedule of committee assignments to be absent from many legislative sessions, allowed Lincoln to represent him. He seemed to be hoping that one day the young man would become the Whig floor leader.

Abe returned home at the end of the

In his first campaign, Abe stood for internal improvements and better education. The high-spirited poster at left heralds an evening speech by candidate A. Lincoln, Esq'r.

legislative session. In spite of the bitter late-February weather, he was in high spirits. Content with the $258 he had drawn for his services and traveling expenses, he resumed his duties as postmaster and surveyor, and returned to the study of law.

New Salem grieved that summer of 1835 over the death of Ann Rutledge, daughter of the former tavern-keeper. Everyone had liked this unaffected girl with her pretty blue eyes and auburn hair. Abe, who once had boarded at her father's tavern, was devoted to the Rutledges, and doubtless to their daughter as well.

When at twenty-two Ann died from a baffling illness (probably typhoid fever), Abe, like many residents of New Salem, was deeply affected. Not until many years later—on February 15, 1862—did the *Menard Axis* of nearby Petersburg create the story about Abe being so much in love with Ann that friends had feared he might attempt suicide. Old-timers in New Salem gave contradictory evidence, some calling the story true, some false. Long after Lincoln's death the story—the myth, truly—that Ann had been his only true love continued to flourish.

Whatever might have happened, the Abe Lincoln who returned to Vandalia in December, 1835, for a special session of the legislature was calm and decisive. Two pressing issues made this session necessary. One was to rush the construction of the Illinois and Michigan Canal. This canal, by

OVERLEAF: *While townspeople gape, a political candidate takes the stump to expound his views in a field outside Bloomington, Indiana, about 1838.*
THE LILLY LIBRARY, INDIANA UNIVERSITY

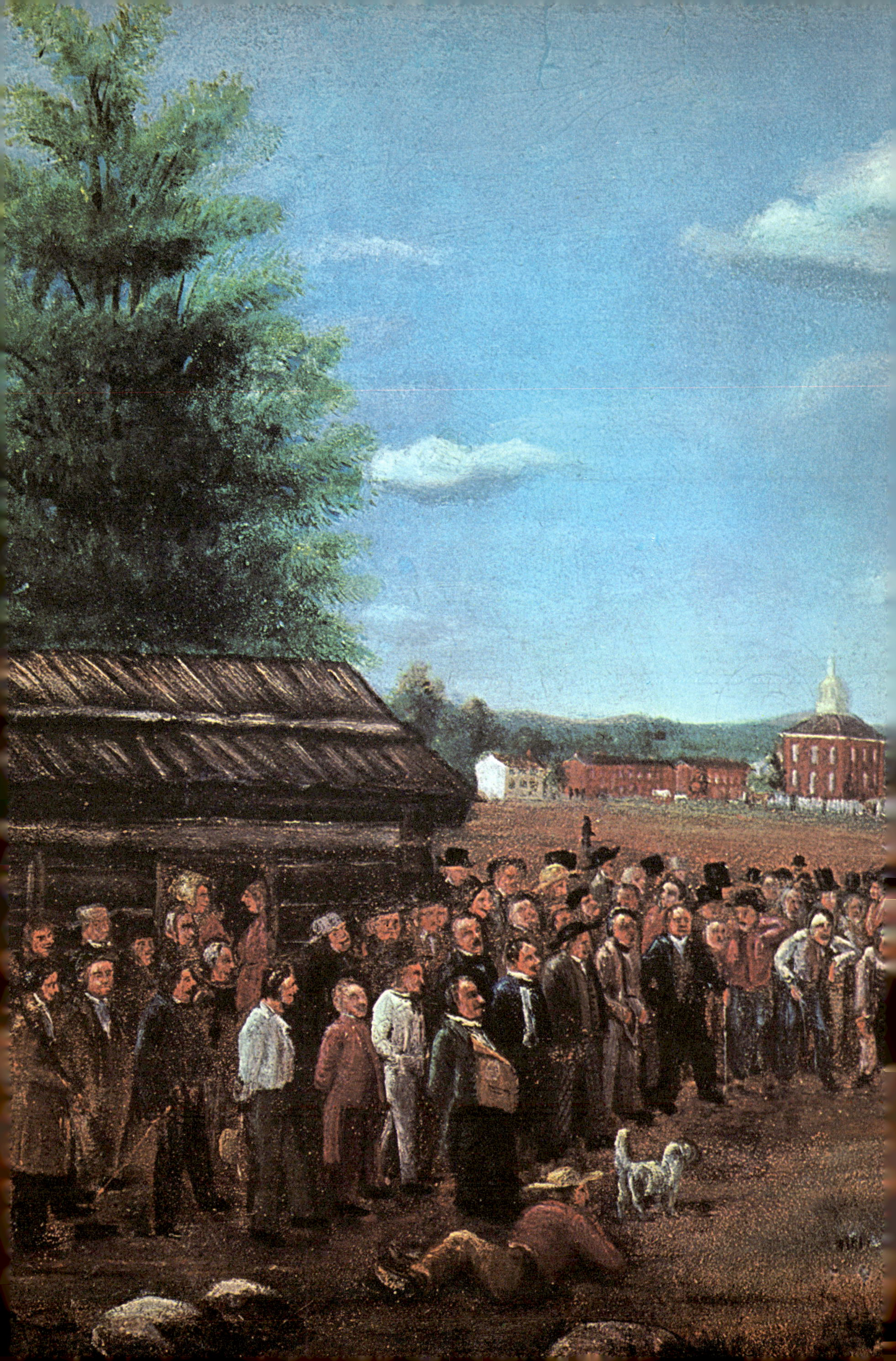

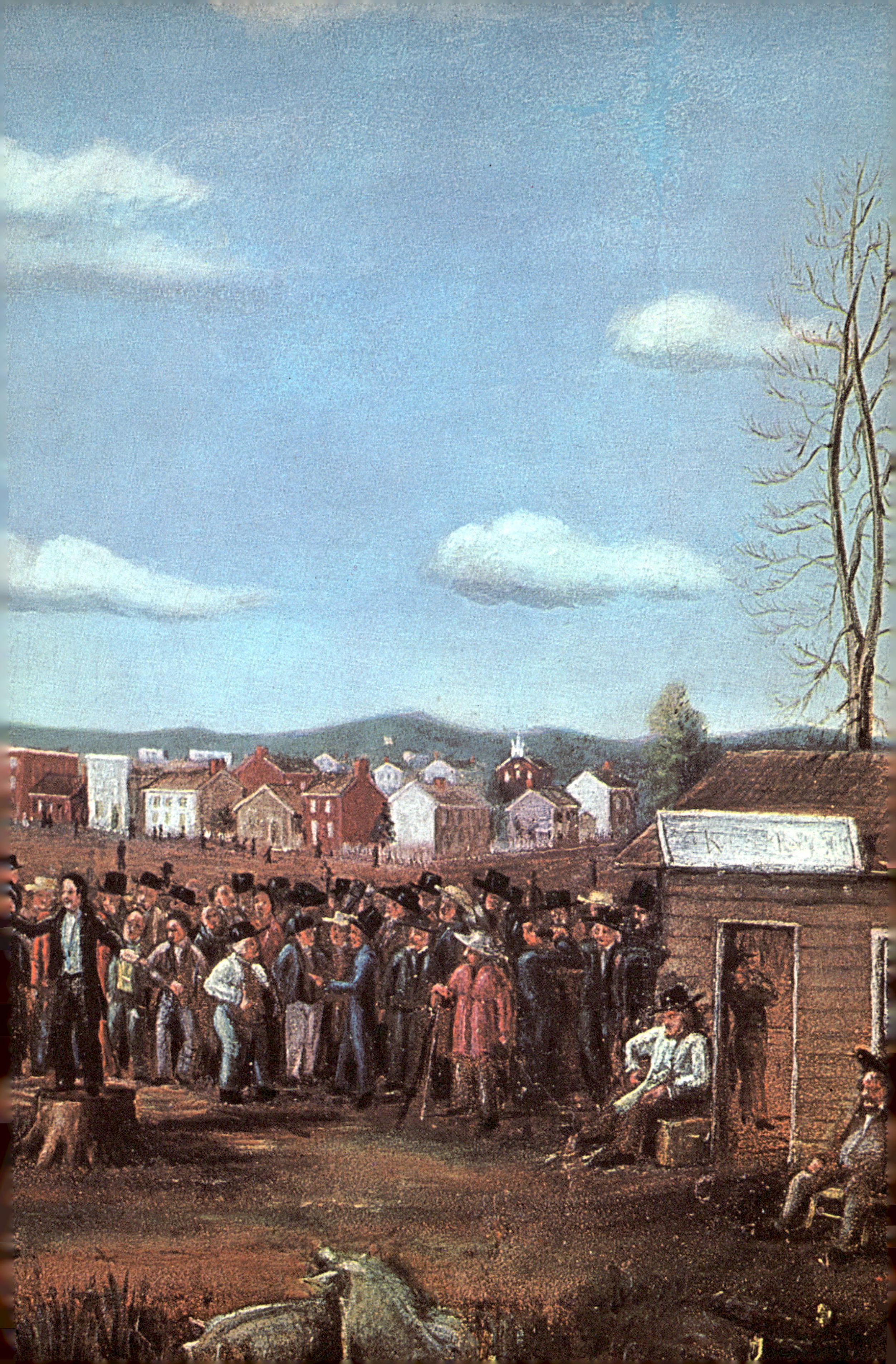

connecting the Illinois River with Lake Michigan, would provide a continuous waterway to the Atlantic via the Great Lakes and the Erie Canal. The second issue was to correct the apportionment of representatives in line with the findings of a new state census. Abe soon learned, however, that work was not to be limited to these two problems. The House alone discussed 139 bills, most of them concerned with the construction of highways and railroads.

Lincoln greatly enjoyed the legislative spree and he took full part in it. He guided through a successful bill to link the Illinois and Michigan Canal to a small canal ending at a townsite near New Salem where he and some friends owned land. In this session Stuart obviously pushed Lincoln forward as Whig floor leader. A national election approached in which Martin Van Buren, as President Jackson's personal choice, could not lose. Lincoln hurried back to New Salem in March, 1836, campaigned vigorously, and won re-election.

Along with Lincoln, Sangamon sent six other representatives and two state senators to Vandalia for the legislative session that convened on December 5, 1836. All were over six feet tall, and they became famous as the Long Nine.

Lincoln became deeply absorbed in the 1836-37 session of the legislature. Political associates, who sometimes called Stuart "Jerry Sly," now recognized how smart he had been in his early choice of a young protégé. Lincoln was described as "the smartest parliamentarian and cunningest 'log-roller'" in a session long-remembered in the history of the Illinois legislature. These unsophisticated legislators believed that money could easily be borrowed to build railroads and canals north and south, east and west. Lincoln and his friends were confident that Illinois would be enriched by every resource—by immigrants, by new towns and cities, by rising land prices, and by industries which would bolster its basic farm economy. One of the most extravagant legislatures in Illinois history was willing to borrow against the future for any internal improvement.

In all the deals that shaped up in the legislature, Lincoln bargained shrewdly. He was committed to moving the state capital to Springfield—closer to the new center of population. But he realized that he would have to overcome the counterclaims of Alton, Decatur, Peoria, Jacksonville, Illiopolis, and Vandalia. Bargaining vote for vote, he won his way.

The institution of slavery also became an issue in this session. Throughout the country abolitionist missionaries had begun to preach strongly worded and highly impassioned sermons against slavery. These preachers and the societies who backed them created violent reactions wherever their message was carried—murderous tempers against abolitionists in the South and among Southern sympathizers, and righteous indignation against slavery in the North.

Illinois was a free state, but the majority of its population had come from the South. These settlers had blood ties as well as business ties in the nearby states of Kentucky and Tennessee. When four Southern states demanded that the North "effectually suppress all associations purporting to be abolition societies," they raised storms of partisan feeling in all the states.

Illinois legislators—more than half of them originally from Kentucky or Tennessee—passed a resolution stating "we highly disapprove of the formation of Abolition societies and of the doctrines promulgated by them ... the right of property in slaves is sacred to the slaveholding States by the Federal Constitution, and ... they cannot be deprived of that right without their consent."

Only two of the Long Nine from Sangamon County refused to support the resolution—Dan Stone and A. Lincoln. They drew up a protest statement hoping it might moderate the issue. Introduced in the legislature on March 3, 1837, it said that "the institution of slavery is founded on both injustice and bad policy, but ... the

This sidewheeler Archimedes *was used to help construct the Illinois and Michigan Canal—one of the many internal improvements which were passed by the Illinois state legislature in which Abe Lincoln served.*

promulgation of abolition doctrines tends rather to increase than abate its evils." They denied the power of Congress "to interfere with the institution of slavery in the different States," but acknowledged the right of Congress "to abolish slavery in the District of Columbia . . . at the request of the people of the District."

1837 was a year filled with disturbing incidents. Outraged Mississippians attacked a number of Negroes accused of planning a slave revolt. A St. Louis mob burned a mulatto who had stabbed a deputy sheriff. Proslavery fanatics in Alton, Illinois, murdered Elijah P. Lovejoy because he insisted on publishing an abolitionist newspaper.

As a would-be lawyer, Abe Lincoln moved steadily ahead. On March 1, 1837, his name was formally endorsed as an attorney. On April 15 a notice in the *Sangamo Journal* announced: "J.T. Stuart and A. Lincoln, Attorneys and Counsellors at Law, will practice conjointly, in the Courts of this Judicial Circuit. Office No. 4 Hoffman's Row upstairs. . . ."

Lincoln packed his personal belongings into a saddlebag and rode into Springfield. Here he obtained lodgings in a room above a store belonging to Joshua Speed, who quickly became a devoted friend. Stuart, it soon developed, was less interested in law than in winning election to Congress—which was no easy contest. He was running for office against one of Illinois's most colorful political fig-

A stagecoach and other vehicles are drawn up in front of the State House in this painting of Vandalia, the capital of Illinois from 1820 to 1839.

HOTEL EVANS, VANDALIA, ILLI

JOHN TODD STUART   STEPHEN T. LOGAN   WILLIAM H. HERNDON

John Stuart, a political ally of Lincoln's, became his law partner in 1837. Strict Judge Logan, Abe's partner from 1841–1844, was his best teacher. The last and best-suited of his law partners was Billy Herndon.

ures, Stephen A. Douglas. Once during the violent campaign they ended a dispute by wrestling on the floor of a store and knocking over the slop jars. When Stuart won the election and departed for Washington in 1839, he was quite content to leave the law business in the hands of the largely untutored Lincoln.

With a firm heart, after seeing Stuart off on the stage, Lincoln wrote across a new page in the firm's account book: "Commencement of Lincoln's administration, 1839. Nov. 2."

The office that Lincoln ran was busy and effective, but it belonged to the easygoing tradition of life on the frontier. Visiting a Sangamon County courtroom in the 1830's, an Eastern attorney shook his head: "To us, just from the city of New York with the sleek lawyers and the prim, dignified judges, with audiences to correspond, there was a contrast so great, that it was almost impossible to repress a burst of laughter. Upon the bench was seated the judge, with his chair tilted back and his heels as high as his head, and in his mouth a veritable corn-cob pipe; his hair standing nine ways for Sunday, while his clothing was more like that worn by a woodchopper than anybody else."

Lincoln came to know many such scenes as he rode from court to court on the Eighth Judicial Circuit, which covered many thousands of square miles. He traveled across the endless prairie enjoying the life of a circuit rider. Court week was a gala time. People came from miles around to hear the cases argued. Afterwards the lawyers met and relaxed, poking fun at one another, telling jokes, and swapping funny stories.

Stuart wrote Lincoln chatty, amia-

Lincoln's law office—marked with an X in this photograph —faced Springfield Square, a muddy road in the heart of town.

ble letters from Washington, yet both knew something was wrong. A young lawyer needed advice, guidance, a chance to grow in knowledge and practice; but Lincoln received professional advice from no one. In a friendly spirit he ended his partnership with Stuart in the spring of 1841, and formed a new partnership with the man who had been so impressed with him during the elections of 1832— Judge Stephen T. Logan.

Ten years Lincoln's senior and former judge of the circuit court, Logan was "a small, thin man, with a little, wrinkled, wizened face, set off by an immense head of hair which might be called frowsy." Where Stuart had been lax, Logan was rigid. His love was law but Logan understood his limitation: his shrill voice was unpleasant and he needed Lincoln for his courtroom orator.

Logan was a driving force that Lincoln would never forget. The judge believed in sources, in authorities, in facts. Day after day he drilled Lincoln on the importance of these methods and principles. Grateful for guidance, Lincoln spent more and more time studying cases. Each new suit Lincoln took to court showed a greater reliance

On the opposite side of the square, partly hidden by trees, stood the County Court House where Lincoln argued his cases.

on evidence and a greater confidence in himself. All at once he was becoming a lawyer in fact as well as in name.

The firm of Logan and Lincoln lasted from 1841 until the fall of 1844 when Logan decided to take his own son into the partnership. Looking around for a new partner, Lincoln recalled William H. Herndon, whom he had known in his first days in Springfield. Everyone called Herndon "Billy," for he wore his informal manner like an old glove. In 1844, Billy was twenty-five, nine years Lincoln's junior. Nothing seemed to suggest that Lincoln should ask Herndon to be his partner. Billy drank where Lincoln never touched liquor; Billy was a strong abolitionist where Lincoln avoided "rabid Yankee influence"; Billy was aggressive where Lincoln sought to smooth out a dispute.

But Lincoln knew the worth of a man. He shared with Billy membership in Springfield's debating and literary society. They had laughed together and each respected the other. Yet as long as their association lasted, Lincoln always called Herndon "Billy," and Herndon always called his partner "Mr. Lincoln."

43

3

MR. LINCOLN GOES TO WASHINGTON

Life in Springfield was often gay and lively. Lincoln was invited to the parties given by the town's best families. At one of these affairs he met Kentucky-born Mary Todd, who had come to live with her sister and brother-in-law, the socially prominent Ninian W. Edwards. "Mary," Edwards remarked, "could make a bishop forget his prayers."

By late summer of 1840, Springfield was gossiping that Lincoln and Mary had reached a serious understanding. Later there was talk that they were to be married on New Year's Day. Then Lincoln lost his nerve, possibly because he was so worn down and dispirited by his hard, lonely life as a circuit rider. He went to see Mary and called off their engagement.

Melancholy fell like a mask across his angular face. He avoided all social engagements for over a year. Yet, even after that length of time, he was upset over gossip that Mary Todd was being courted by an attractive widower.

Finally, Mrs. Simeon Francis, wife of the editor of the *Sangamo Journal* and one of Lincoln's closest friends, arranged for the couple to meet unexpectedly. Other meetings followed, often in the company of bright-eyed Julia Jayne, who was as interested in Whig politics as Mary. The two girls soon had Lincoln deeply involved in a piece of rascality.

James Shields, a quick-tempered Irish Democrat, was serving Illinois at this time as State Auditor. Shields, knowing that the state's indebtedness had pushed down the value of notes issued by the State Bank, ordered the state's collector of revenue to credit State Bank notes at only forty-four cents on the dollar.

Citizens of Illinois were incensed by this move, and Whigs like Lincoln, Mary, and Julia decided to make polit-

Lincoln was first photographed by a traveling daguerreotype artist in 1846. Despite a slight stiffness, due to his holding a long pose, the successful legislator and promising lawyer looked poised and confident.

44

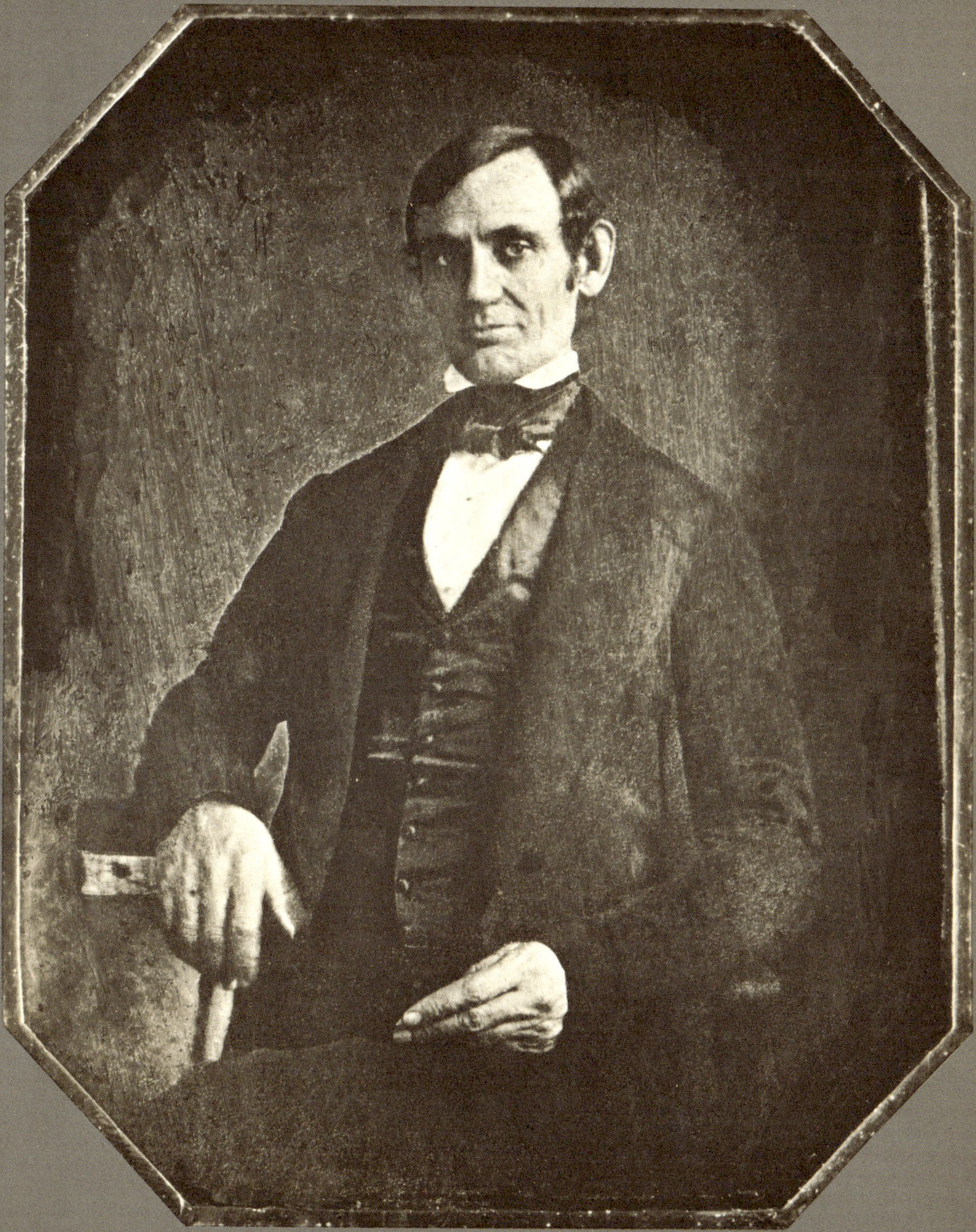

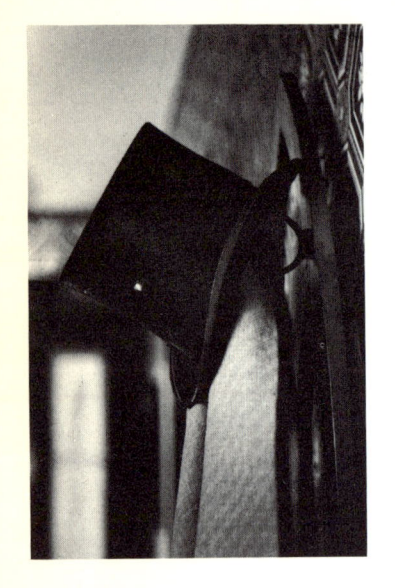

The sociable but formal life that people led in Springfield in the 1840's is shown in these photographs of the restored Lincoln home. At right is the parlor; below is Mr. Lincoln's desk with his spectacles; at the far left, his stovepipe hat hangs as if he were just about to return to reclaim it at the next stroke of the clock.

ical gain from this discontent. A series of letters began to appear in the *Sangamo Journal*, apparently written by a widow named Rebecca, ridiculing Shields's conduct. The third letter, outrageously insisting that Shields must be a Whig "since no Democrat would be so faithless with the people," had the unmistakable tone of Lincoln's biting wit.

Lincoln's humor was hearty, but it also had a sharp edge. Shields, who had a delicate sense of honor, was deeply offended by the letters and challenged Lincoln to a duel.

Although Lincoln was riding the circuit, Shields was determined to challenge him to a duel, and followed him relentlessly. Lincoln at first offered to acknowledge that he had written the letters out of purely political—not personal—motives. But then he realized that in a situation of wounded pride, humor might be a better solution than a bloody duel. Since he had been challenged, he had the right to choose the weapons. Lincoln's selection and terms were so ludicrous that the affair became a comedy. Let the duel be fought, Lincoln announced, with the largest of all cavalry broadswords within a space that would allow neither man to retreat more than eight feet. Since Shields was short, and Lincoln exceptionally tall, the prospect of such a fight became absurd. When the two men met on the dueling ground near Alton the affair was speedily patched up.

However, the romance and danger of the Shields affair drew Lincoln still closer to Mary. On the morning of November 4, 1842, Lincoln announced to his future-brother-in-law that he planned to marry Miss Todd that very day. This surprising news threw the Edwards household into a frenzy of preparation. That evening, by candle-

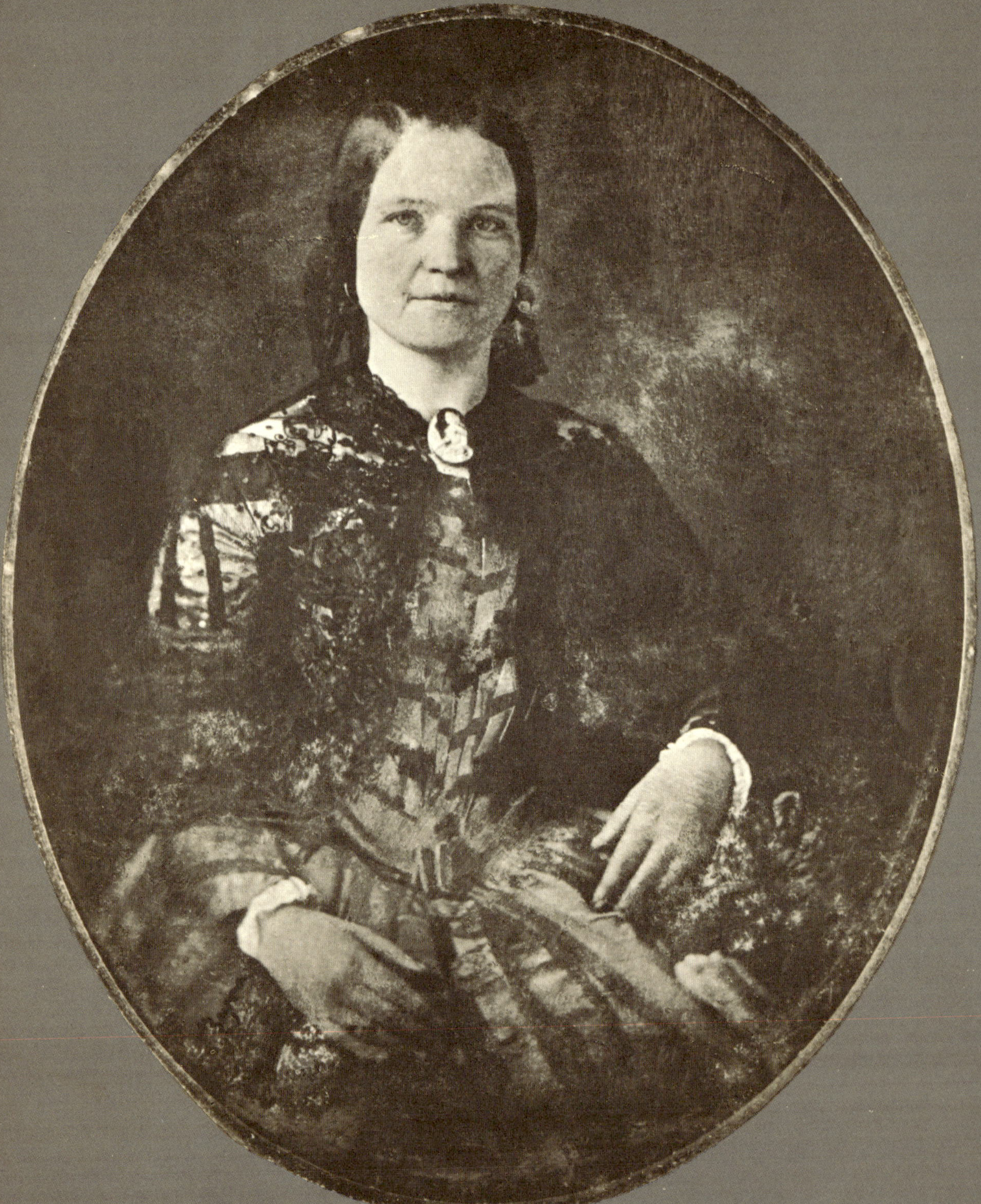

light, Lincoln and Mary exchanged vows. "Nothing new here," Lincoln wrote a fellow lawyer soon afterward, "except my marrying, which, to me, is a matter of profound wonder."

The couple lived modestly in the Globe Tavern, where on August 1, 1843, Robert Todd Lincoln was born. Soon after his birth the Lincolns purchased a large frame house on the corner of Eighth and Jackson streets, some five blocks southeast of the business district, where they lived during their remaining years in Springfield. Their second son, Edward Baker Lincoln, was born three years later.

Since he had served four terms in the state legislature, Lincoln felt that he was ready to try for a congressional seat in the elections of 1843. But he was not the only able young lawyer in Illinois who had political ambitions. He had to wait until 1846 for the Whig nomination. His opponent, Peter Cartwright, a famous Methodist minister of the region, fought a hard campaign, but Lincoln won by a landslide. In late October of 1847, with his family, he boarded the stage that carried them to Mrs. Lincoln's family home in Lexington, Kentucky. After a short visit, they continued on to the nation's capital.

Washington was a city liberally dotted with pigsties, privies, and refuse-filled alleyways. Moreover it was cold and damp in winter, and unbearably humid in summer. Mrs. Lincoln tried to endure life in the capital, but was soon defeated. She holed up in a room, refusing to go anywhere or to meet anyone. With good sense Lincoln sent her and the children back to Lexington.

Yet, in his way, Lincoln was happy in Washington. He took rooms in Mrs. Sprigg's boardinghouse, and his tales and jokes delighted the other boarders gathered at Mrs. Sprigg's table.

Lincoln's seat in the very center of the back row on the Whig side of the House was one of the worst. Yet Lincoln, always a hard worker, threw himself wholeheartedly into his legislative labors. He clung with unflinching loyalty to Whig policies when Democratic President Polk attempted to justify the Mexican War by insisting that the first blood had been shed on American soil. Lincoln answered with a speech calling on the President to prove beyond doubt that the "spot" where the war had started had not been a part of Mexico. In a resolution of thanks to General Zachary Taylor for the victory at Buena Vista, Lincoln was among the Whigs who voted for an amendment protesting that the war was "unconstitutionally and unnecessarily begun by the President."

Such political maneuvering may have been great legislative sport in Washington. But in Illinois, where the land-hungry pioneers strongly supported the war, Lincoln's actions

Wearing a fashionable dress, her hair demurely arranged in curls at her neck, Mary Todd Lincoln sat for this portrait in 1846. A vivacious, charming woman at social gatherings, she suffered from blinding headaches and violent attacks of hysteria in later years.

aroused deep resentment. Democratic newspapers derisively nicknamed him "Spotty" Lincoln.

On the other hand, issues that could be brushed aside in Illinois suddenly acquired vitality in Washington. Slaves, chained together into long lines, were frequently driven through the streets of the capital. Deeply upset, Lincoln described a "sort of Negro livery-stable" he had once seen where "droves of Negroes were collected . . . precisely like droves of horses" for shipment to Southern markets.

Lincoln found himself agreeing with David Wilmot, a Democrat from Pennsylvania, who had disrupted the session by introducing his famous proviso forbidding the extension of slavery into any territory gained as a result of the Mexican War. Bitter battle lines were being drawn.

During these legislative skirmishes, Lincoln was lonely for his family, and missed them deeply. He and Mrs. Lincoln exchanged frequent, affectionate letters—he sending copies of his speeches, she keeping him informed on the doings of his adored sons.

Meanwhile a presidential election was approaching, and the Whigs felt strong enough to win. Since their only other successful candidate had been a war hero, General William Henry Harrison, they decided to stick with the military. Overlooking their acknowledged leader, Henry Clay, for a second time, the Whigs nominated General Zachary Taylor. "Old Rough and Ready" was an opinionated, aggressive man, but as the victor of the Battle of Buena Vista, he was a magnificent vote-getter.

Lincoln attended the nominating convention in Philadelphia in June, 1848, and pledged himself to Taylor's campaign. After making a rousing speech at a Whig rally in Chicago, he campaigned for two weeks on his home ground. Because of his anti-war record, Lincoln was decidedly unpopular with the flag-waving patriots of Illinois—one of the reasons he was not up for re-election himself. Yet, largely due to his efforts, Lincoln's congressional district contributed a solid majority to Taylor's national success.

Lincoln returned to Washington in

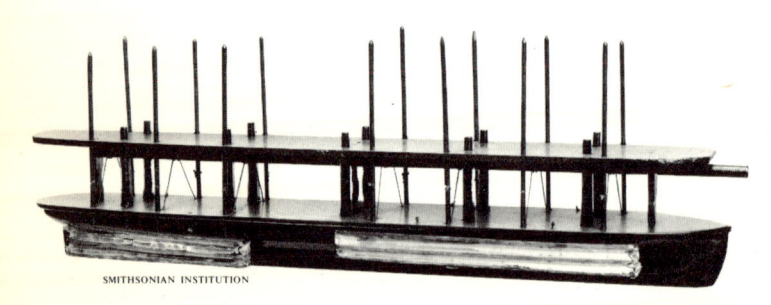

In Washington, Lincoln registered an invention with the Patent Office—a device to lift ships over shoals (model at left). The ship was lifted by "buoyant chambers" that were forced under the hull by vertical spars.

SMITHSONIAN INSTITUTION

50

The U.S. provoked the Mexican War in the opinion of certain Whigs, Lincoln included. The Whig champion Daniel Webster is shown in this cartoon defending his right to make such a charge against President Polk (at left).

December for the second session of the Thirtieth Congress. The end of the Mexican War had finally brought the issue of slavery into the open. Party lines disappeared. Northern Whigs and Democrats voted together against the extension of slavery. Southerners presented a solid front of opposition to any criticism of their "peculiar institution."

In later years Lincoln claimed that he voted at least forty times for various versions of the Wilmot Proviso. The difficulties brought up by the proviso were the admission of California as a free state; the admission of New Mexico (also likely to become a free state); the settlement of the boundary dispute between New Mexico and Texas (a slave state); and the regulation of the slave trade carried on within the District of Columbia.

51

THE SINGSONG PARTY

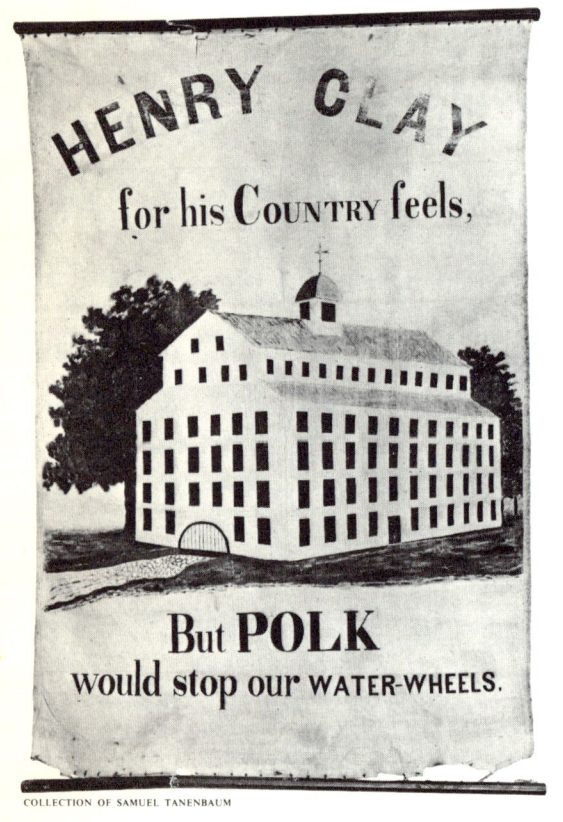

HENRY CLAY for his Country feels, But POLK would stop our WATER-WHEELS.

COLLECTION OF SAMUEL TANENBAUM

OLD PRINT SHOP

TAYLOR

The Whigs were masters at winning elections by means of cider and song—earning the nickname of the "Singsong Party." The 1840 songsheet at right sings the praises of William H. Harrison. The painting above shows the effects of cider on voters lining up to register. In 1844 Henry Clay used these beguiling tactics, plus support for American industry (poster, upper left), but lost because he opposed the Mexican War. In 1848 the Whigs helped their last presidential candidate, Zachary Taylor, into office by using martial posters like that at far left.

Lincoln, silent and thoughtful, finally announced his intention to offer a bill abolishing the slave trade in the District of Columbia. The bill proposed that all children born to slave mothers after January 1, 1850, were to be set free and apprenticed to learn a trade. It also proposed that other slaves be emancipated voluntarily by their owners who would then receive adequate compensation. Lincoln made both these provisions subject to the consent of the citizens of the District. But after counting up the supporting votes he could get, he realized it could not possibly pass. Sadly, he shelved the bill.

Tension continued to mount in the debates of the Thirtieth Congress. Led by South Carolina's militant orator, John C. Calhoun, Southerners accused the North of aggression toward them, toward their property, toward their way of life. They demanded full protection for their constitutional right to take their own personal property—whether cattle, furniture, or slaves—wherever they moved. In addition, they demanded the enactment of a Fugitive Slave Law that would force Northerners to return escaping slaves, and they called for an immediate end to all abolitionist agitation.

Toward the end of the session, Southern forces tried to push through the Walker Amendment which would extend slavery to the new territories. Debates on the issue were very bitter and fists flew. But an alliance of Northern Whigs and free-soil Democrats managed to kill the measure.

When Lincoln's term ended in the spring of 1849, he had no desire to leave the political whirl of Washington. For some months he remained in the capital attempting to use his waning influence to recommend Whig appointments from Illinois. Lincoln tried his only case before the Supreme Court—and lost; and he applied for a patent on his own invention, a device to lift boats over shoals and sandbars. A political dispute over an appointment in the General Land Office called for a quick trip to Springfield. But he was back in Washington soon after, lobbying for the position himself.

Disappointed in all but the patent, Lincoln sadly moved himself and his family back to their house in Springfield. Adding to his distress, his youngest boy, Eddy, fell ill and died. Billy Herndon remarked that "melancholy dripped from him when he walked."

Intimate friends sensed the profound change that Washington had made in Lincoln. Always an introspective man, he seemed now to be continually lost in his own thoughts. It was as though he had decided that the career of A. Lincoln, public servant, had come to an end, and a new career for A. Lincoln, private citizen, had begun.

A window in Lincoln's office in Springfield overlooked the Sangamon County Courthouse which then housed the state legislature. Atop the dome flies the American flag which Lincoln had only just begun to serve.

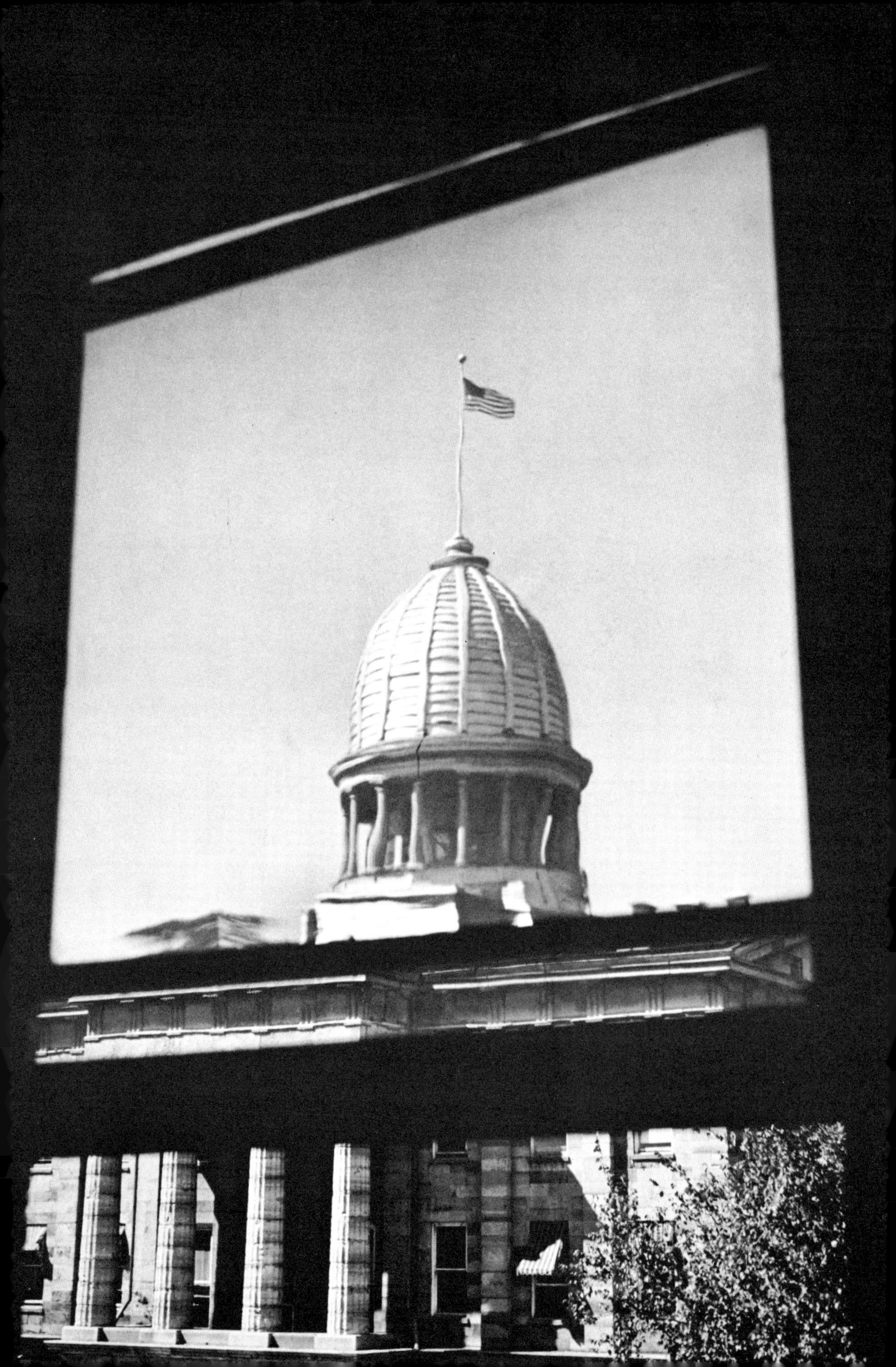

4 THE GREAT DEBATE

Zachary Taylor, owing some favor for Lincoln's support during the presidential canvass, offered him the governorship of the Oregon Territory. Lincoln declined, reconciled to putting politics aside as he concentrated on his career as a successful lawyer.

In Lincoln's mind, the Compromise of 1850 solved the turmoil over slavery brought about by the Mexican War and the failure of the Wilmot Proviso. The compromise, worked out by Henry Clay, Stephen A. Douglas, and Daniel Webster, had been designed to smooth out the differences between the North and the South. It provided for the admission of California as a free state, the settlement of the Texas–New Mexico border dispute, and the admission of New Mexico and Utah as territories where "popular sovereignty" would decide the question of slavery.

Lincoln was pleased by another provision that called for an end to the slave trade in the District of Colum-

The Compromise of 1850 was a masterful stroke of statesmanship that temporarily resolved which new states would be free and which slave. A packed Senate chamber (right) hears Henry Clay propose the Compromise.

LIBRARY OF CONGRESS

Two courtrooms on the Illinois' Eighth Judicial Circuit are seen above: the upstairs room of a log structure at Decatur, and Mt. Pulaski's more civilized court chamber, built in 1847.

bia. But he was grieved that a stringent Fugitive Slave Law was the price of the measure.

After his return from Washington, fellow lawyers grumbled over Lincoln's moodiness and his dedication to books. Between cases they found him studying mathematics and astronomy, and enjoying the works of Shakespeare. Yet to Isaac N. Arnold, who knew him as well as anyone, Lincoln was unspoiled. Describing his friend's appearance at forty, Arnold saw "a very tall specimen of that type of long, large-boned man produced in the northern part of the Mississippi Valley.... He would have been instantly recognized as a Western man, and his stature, figure, dress, manner, voice, and accent indicated that he was from the Northwest. In manner he was cordial, frank, and friendly, and, although not without dignity, he put every one perfectly at ease."

For six months of every year Lincoln traveled the many counties comprising the vast domain of the Eighth Judicial Circuit. He saw the once-empty prairie begin to change. He rode past frame dwellings that had replaced the old log cabins. He watched horses instead of oxen pull steel-clad plows through the sod. But some things never changed. The winters were still cruelly cold, and the spring rains still turned the countryside into oceans of mud. Yet Lincoln drifted back into the old hardships without

58

complaint. He rode the circuit "behind his own horse, which was an indifferent, rawboned specimen, in his own blacksmith-made buggy."

Lincoln's practice grew steadily. He won renown as an outstanding lawyer who handled both important cases and small cases, giving to each his best efforts. One of the high points in Lincoln's legal career was the case in which he defended the Illinois Central Railroad from taxes assessed by officials in one county. It was a case of national significance, and Lincoln's defense showed him to be a shrewd and forceful advocate.

Yet he remained moody and remote. Fortunately, his law partner, Billy Herndon, fitted Lincoln's moods. The younger man did not mind the chaos of the office or Lincoln's informality. John H. Littlefield, who studied law under the pair, wrote: "There was no order in the office at all. The firm of Lincoln and Herndon kept no books. They divided their fees without taking any receipts or making any entries on books. One day Mr. Lincoln received $5,000 as a fee in a railroad case [the Illinois Central settlement]. He came in and said: 'Well, Billy,' addressing his partner, Mr. Herndon, 'here is our fee; sit down and let me divide.' He counted out $2,500 to his partner, and gave it to him with as much nonchalance as he would have given a few cents for a paper."

Among his most celebrated trials was his defense of Duff Armstrong, son of the Jack Armstrong whom Lincoln had beaten in the wrestling match long before in New Salem. Duff was accused of murdering a man named Metzker at a camp meeting in 1857. He pleaded innocent although the State's star witness testified that he had seen Duff strike the fatal blow.

Abe had rocked the cradle in which Duff had lain as a babe and Hannah Armstrong, Duff's mother, had patched Abe Lincoln's pants. With these memories, Lincoln arose to defend young Armstrong. When, he asked the troublesome eyewitness, had the fatal attack occurred? Answer: About eleven o'clock at night. Ques-

A court-week crowd gawks as Lincoln and his colleagues ride into town. Because of the Springfield attorney's popularity, the new seat of Logan County was named Lincoln.

59

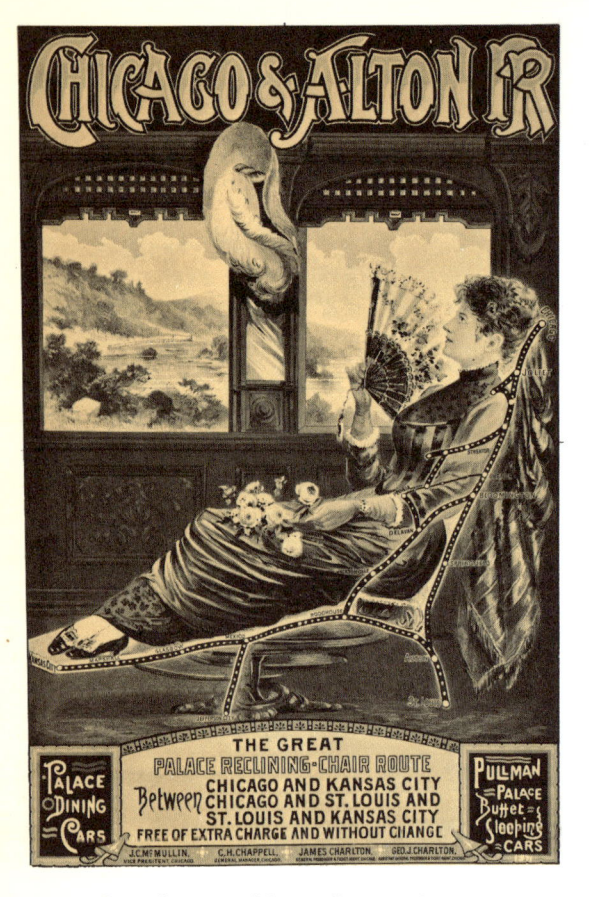

Lincoln earned large fees in the 1850's by handling cases for railroads such as the Chicago & Alton, whose Palace Reclining-Chair Route is advertised in the poster above.

tion: How far had the witness stood from the scene of the crime? Answer: About one hundred and fifty feet. Question: How had the witness been able, at this distance, to recognize the details of the crime? Answer: A full moon had made the scene as bright as midday.

This was the moment for which Lincoln had been waiting. He introduced into evidence an almanac proving that on the night in question only a quarter-moon had shone. No one could have witnessed the crime under the circumstances stated. In shirt sleeves with one suspender strap hanging off his shoulder, Lincoln addressed the jury. Tears streaked his face at the end of his brilliant and moving speech. When the jury left the courtroom, he whispered to Duff's mother: "They'll clear him before dark, Hannah." He was acquitted on the first ballot.

Perhaps Lincoln was reasonably content with his life at this time. Judge David Davis, one of the liveliest gentlemen on the Eighth Judicial Circuit, insisted that "Lincoln was happy, as happy as *he* could be, when on this circuit and happy no other place."

Was the statement true? There was lively gossip about Lincoln's home life. One story told about Mrs. Lincoln chasing him from the house with a broom. Another had her pouring water on his head from a second-story window to keep him from tracking up the floor. A third had him standing at the front door shouting at his wife: "You make the house intolerable, damn you, get out of it!" Did truth support these tales?

When they were first married, Lincoln's nickname for Mary was "Molly." By the time of Willie's birth in late 1850, and Tad's birth in April, 1853, he was calling her "Mother." Mary Lincoln was a proud, high-strung woman. Few servants could stand her tongue-lashings for long. She suffered headaches and bad dreams resulting, in

The emotional quality of Lincoln's famous defense of Duff Armstrong is captured in this lithograph—although many details are inaccurate. Lincoln had not grown a beard at that time and did not address the country jury so formally.

later years, in a mental illness approaching insanity. But no one understood her better or was more willing to forgive her faults than her husband. When little Eddie died in 1850, his mother had been wracked with grief. If her temper had quickened thereafter, terrifying servants and delivery boys, Lincoln knew why.

Billy Herndon, who never liked Mrs. Lincoln, described her harshly in later years: "It was the habit, custom, of Mrs. Lincoln, when any big man or woman visited her house, to dress up and trot out Bob, Willie, or Tad and get them to monkey around, talk, dance, speak, quote poetry, etc., etc. Then she would become enthusiastic and eloquent over the children, much to the annoyance of the visitor and to the mortification of Lincoln. However, Lincoln was totally blind to his children's faults. . . . He, Lincoln, used to come down to our office on Sunday when Mrs. Lincoln had gone to church, *to show her new bonnet.* . . . Lincoln would turn Willie and Tad loose in our office, and they soon gutted the room, gutted the shelves of books, rifled the drawers, and riddled boxes, battered the points of my gold pens against the stairs, turned over the inkstands on the papers, scattered letters over the office, and danced over them and the like. I have felt many a time that I wanted to wring the necks of these brats and pitch them out of the windows, but out of respect for Lincoln and knowing that he was abstracted, I shut my mouth, bit my lips, and left for parts unknown."

Absorbed in the problems of an expanding law practice and growing family, Lincoln seemed indifferent toward politics. He sent Herndon to discourage his nomination for the state legislature in 1852, and showed no interest in the suggestion that he run for governor. The Whig candidate for President—Winfield Scott, another hero of the Mexican War—drew several short speeches from Lincoln, but none of the passionate feeling with which he had gone campaigning for

Armed, disorderly men rampage toward Lawrence, Kansas. These border ruffians hoped to win Lawrence and the entire territory of "Bloody Kansas" for slaveholders.

History of Kansas, HOLLOWAY, 1868

Taylor. The Democratic candidate, Franklin Pierce of New Hampshire, defeated Scott roundly.

Yet as 1853 wore on, and Lincoln read the newspapers, his indifferent attitude changed. For the third time California delayed the deadline for removing slaves from its territory. There were persistent rumors of a Southern plot to seize Spanish-held Cuba. And President Pierce was proving himself a weak man, who could be easily swayed by the arguments of powerful Southerners. It became increasingly apparent to Lincoln that Southern slave interests were rapidly gaining control over the affairs of the nation.

Lincoln's attention focused on Stephen A. Douglas, who had come to Illinois from Vermont. A small man, but forceful and ambitious, Douglas had fought his way upward in Democratic politics to a judgeship. He had moved on to the House of Representatives and then to the Senate where devoted friends called him "the Little Giant." His years in Washington had given Douglas polish, confidence, a sense of destiny. In 1854 he assumed the chairmanship of the Senate's powerful Committee on Territories. He sponsored several bills which provided for the formation of Nebraska as a free territory, and Kansas as a slave territory. In effect, these bills canceled out the Missouri Compromise of 1820 which forbade slavery in the Louisiana Territory north of 36°30′. Eventually Douglas called for the repeal of the Compromise itself.

When Lincoln heard of this in Springfield, he awoke as though jolted by an electric shock. He plunged back into politics by taking the stump for Richard Yates, who was running for re-election to Congress in vigorous opposition to the Kansas–Nebraska Bill.

Lincoln ended the campaign for Yates at the State Fair in Springfield where he stood in shirt sleeves addressing a large crowd. He denounced the Kansas–Nebraska Bill as illegal since it violated both the will of the people and the Constitution by extending slavery into new territory. Let slavery stay where it was, Lincoln argued—time would kill it.

His thin, high-pitched voice reached out to the audience. His face grew radiant, and his awkward gestures became extensions of his thought. Hearing Lincoln that day, Herndon was galvanized into action. He hurried his partner out of town before he could be taken into the camp of the radical abolitionists.

Lincoln's rousing speech was the mature expression of his lifelong feelings toward slavery. In August of 1855 he wrote to his old friend Joshua Speed recalling: "In 1841 you and I had together a tedious low-water trip on a steamboat from Louisville to St. Louis. You may remember, as I well do, that from Louisville to the mouth of the Ohio there were on board ten or a dozen slaves shackled together with irons. That sight was a continued torment to me, and I see something like it every time I touch the Ohio or any other slave border."

Lincoln realized that his beliefs had gone beyond the confines of Whig policy. Billy Herndon, describing his partner's quandary, said Lincoln knew "that if he expected to figure as a leader he must take a stand himself. Mere hatred of slavery and opposition to the injustice of the Kansas–Nebraska legislation were not all that were required of him. He must be a Democrat, Know-Nothing, Abolitionist, or Republican. . . . At length he declared himself."

The anti-slavery factions united in the Republican Party, formed in 1854. At the approach of the presidential election of 1856, Illinois Republicans organized themselves and held their first state convention in May at Bloomington. All sorts of people attended: disenchanted Whigs, abolitionists, free-soilers, Democrats who opposed the Kansas–Nebraska Act, and prominent businessmen looking for a strong central government that would protect their interests. With high hopes for the success of the new party, Lincoln and Herndon also came to town.

Repeated calls came for Lincoln to speak. Unfortunately, no copy of the remarks he made exists, but to Herndon, Lincoln's "Lost Speech" at Bloomington was the "grand effort of his life. . . . If Mr. Lincoln was six feet, four inches high usually, at Bloomington that day he was seven feet, and inspired at that. From that day to the day of his death he stood firm in the right. He felt his great cross, had his great idea, nursed it, kept it, taught it to others, in his fidelity bore witness of it to his death, and finally sealed it with his precious blood." A roar of applause went up as Lincoln finished his speech.

When the Republican National Convention opened in Philadelphia the following month, it was obvious that Lincoln had not been forgotten. John C. Frémont, the famous explorer of the West, was nominated for President. Then the hassle over the vice-presidential candidate began. In Urbana, where Lincoln was finishing some cases, a fellow lawyer rushed up with the exciting news that Lincoln had received 110 votes, and stood second in an informal balloting for Vice-President. "I reckon that ain't me," Lincoln replied indifferently. "There's another great man in Massachusetts named Lincoln, and I reckon it's him."

But Abraham Lincoln of Illinois had indeed been the man many of the delegates in Philadelphia had wanted. Believing that the new party could resolve the differences threatening the Union, Lincoln campaigned vigorously for the Republican candidates in 1856. One of his speeches impressed Noah Brooks, a young newspaperman, who remembered "a choleric old Democrat striding away from an open-air meeting where Lincoln was speaking, striking the earth with his

FREE STATES
SLAVE STATES
TERRITORIES

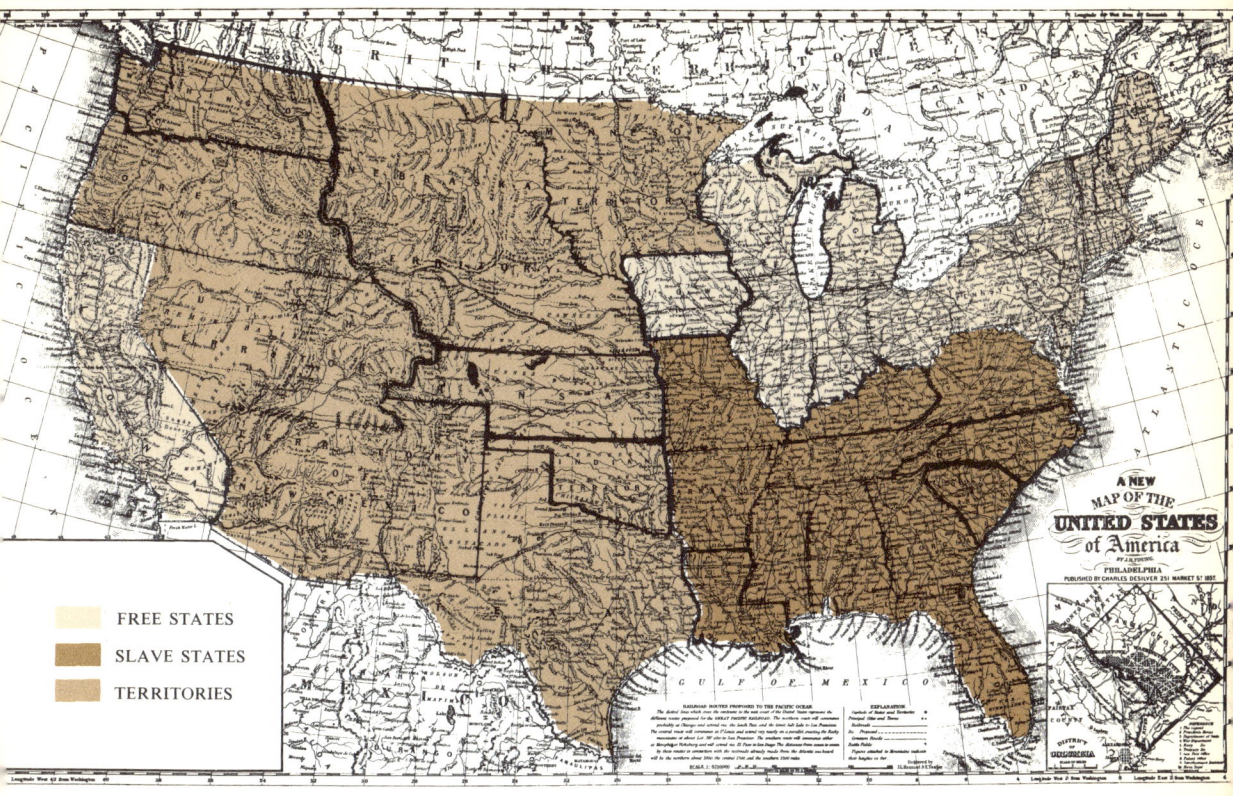

THE FREE AND THE SLAVE

As the election of 1856 neared, the United States was bitterly divided (above) between free and slave states. Some of the territories (notably Oregon which went "free" in 1848) had declared themselves, but in others the choice was still open. The Republicans, in their 1856 platform, gave Americans their first chance to vote against extending slavery in the territories. The eagle on the poster at right carries a banner proclaiming "Freedom for Kansas!" But the Republicans lost, partly because the party was not yet strongly organized, and partly because their candidate, Frémont, was more of a hero than he was a seasoned politician.

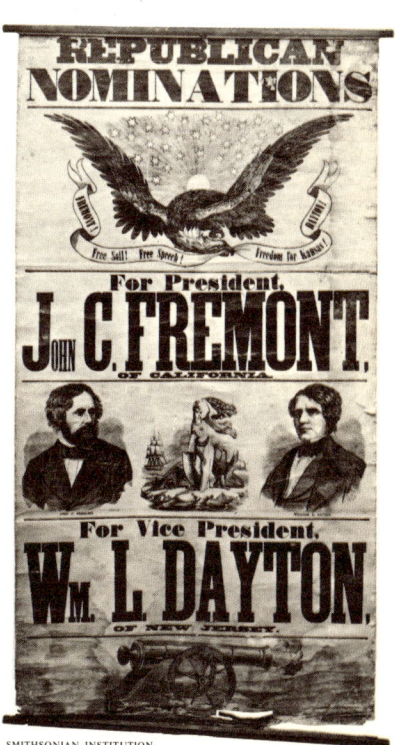

ROGER B. TANEY DRED SCOTT

A slave family dashes for freedom in the dramatic painting below, made just before the Civil War by Eastman Johnson. Dred Scott (above right) sued for his freedom from slavery in the Supreme Court only to have Chief Justice Roger Taney (above left) deny all Negroes their Constitutional rights.

cane as he stumped along and exclaiming, 'He's a dangerous man, sir! a damned dangerous man! He makes you believe what he says, in spite of yourself!'"

James Buchanan, the Democratic candidate, managed to win the presidency. But the Republicans showed surprising strength. They carried all but four of the Northern states. Two days after Buchanan's inauguration, a packed courtroom waited for the decision of the United States Supreme Court in the Dred Scott case. Scott, a Negro slave, was suing for his freedom on the ground that he had been taken by his master into a territory where the Missouri Compromise prohibited slavery.

Chief Justice Roger B. Taney delivered the majority opinion in a funereal voice. He shocked the crowd in the courtroom by declaring that at the time the Constitution was adopted Negroes "had no rights which the white man was bound to respect." Therefore, the justice continued, since Negroes were not citizens of the United States, they had no right to sue in a Federal court. Going even further, he declared the Missouri Compromise unconstitutional and denied the right of Congress, or any territorial legislature to prohibit slavery.

Lincoln was flabbergasted—the Dred Scott decision shook the foundations of his belief that slavery could never be extended. In June of 1858, as the "first and only choice" of Illinois Republicans for the United States Senate, Lincoln opposed Stephen A. Douglas, defender of Taney's decision. When Lincoln read his acceptance speech to leaders of his party, he drew comments ranging from the remarks that the speech was "ahead of its time" and a "damned fool utterance," to Herndon's avowed assertion: "Lincoln, deliver that speech as read and it will make you President."

Delivering the speech "as read," Lincoln said: "We are now far into the *fifth* year since a policy was initiated with the *avowed* object, and *confident* promise, of putting an end to slavery agitation.

". . . Under the operation of that policy, that agitation has not only *not ceased,* but has *constantly augmented.*

"In *my* opinion, it *will* not cease, until a *crisis* shall have been reached, and passed.

"'A house divided against itself cannot stand.'

"I believe this government cannot endure, permanently half *slave* and half *free.*

"I do not expect the Union to be *dissolved*—I do not expect the house to *fall*—but I *do* expect it will cease to be divided.

"It will become *all* one thing, or *all* the other. . . ."

The eloquence and passionate sincerity of the speech was evident to all who heard or read it—including Douglas. He opened his campaign in a fighting mood in Chicago three weeks after Lincoln made his "House

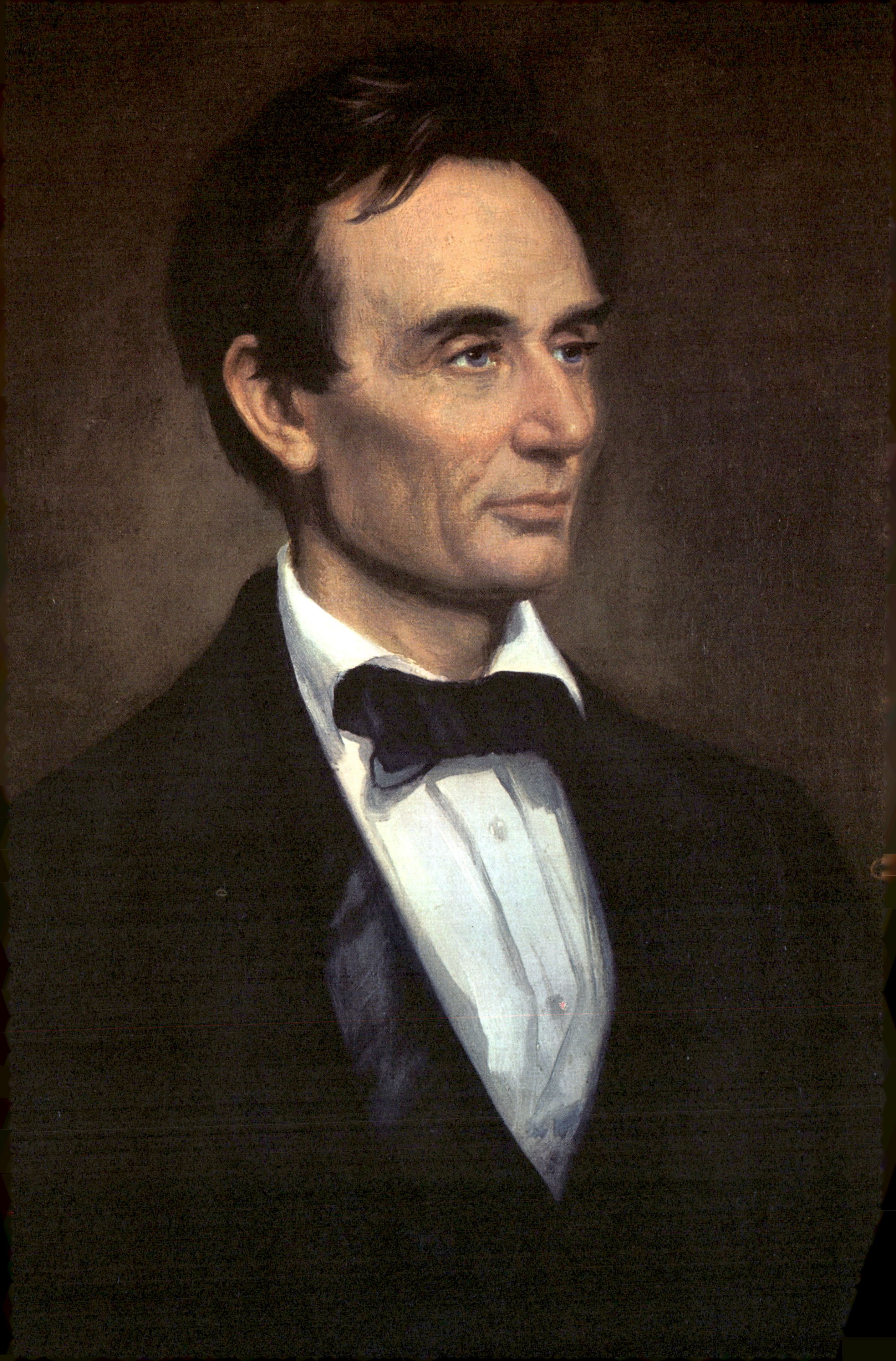

Divided" speech. Lincoln replied the following night, and both candidates spoke to audiences in Springfield ten days later. Partly by accident and partly by Lincoln's planning, the campaign assumed the pattern of a debate. Lincoln now proposed to formalize this pattern and extend it to confrontations all around the state. Douglas accepted the challenge, although he did not deny that Lincoln would make a dangerous adversary. "I shall have my hands full," the judge said. "He is the strong man of his party—full of wit, facts, dates—and the best stump speaker . . . in the West."

The first scheduled debate occurred on August 21, 1858, in Ottawa, Illinois. Douglas was to open with a speech of an hour's duration, Lincoln was to take an hour and a half for his reply, and Douglas would close in thirty minutes. Thereafter the rivals would take turns in leading the discussions.

Never again would "Ottoway" see the likes of that bright August day when Stephen A. Douglas, national statesman, met Abraham Lincoln, prairie politician, for the first time. From sunrise to noon six thousand persons crushed their way into town. A special train of seventeen cars brought visitors from Chicago. Bands played on street corners, and buildings were gaily decorated with bunting.

The debate, delivered from a platform in the public square, found Douglas following a familiar argument: "I hold that . . . each and every state of this Union is a sovereign power, with the right to do as it pleases upon this question of slavery, and upon all its domestic institutions."

Lincoln hit back hard: "When he [Douglas] says he 'cares not whether slavery is voted down or voted up'— that it is a sacred right of self government—he is in my judgment penetrating the human soul and eradicating the light of reason and the love of liberty in this American people."

Cheers, laughter, applause, and shouts of "Good for you!" "That's so!" and "We stand by that!" greeted

Lincoln's eloquence first won national notice in his "House Divided" speech, recalled in the 1861 cartoon at right. Yet politicians felt his ungainly looks could only be overcome by commissioning such idealized portraits as the one by G.P.A. Healy at left.

Frank Leslie's Illustrated Newspaper, FEBRUARY 2, 1861

THE MESERVE COLLECTION

the vigorous remarks of both men. Both candidates were satisfied with their performances, and Lincoln said amiably, "The fire flew some, and I am glad to know that I am yet alive."

In spite of wild newspaper stories —slanted obviously toward Lincoln or toward Douglas—the debate acquired a profound national meaning as the two men swung up and down and back and forth across Illinois. Other topics could easily have occupied their time—immigration, the tariff, the opening of new land to homesteaders, or safeguards against depression. But these two canny, witty, experienced orators chose instead to deal with the issue of slavery in the territories.

In the last debate, held in Alton, Lincoln summed up what he felt to be the heart of the debate. "The real issue in this controversy—the one pressing upon every mind—is the sentiment on the part of one class that looks upon the institution of slavery *as a wrong*, and of another class that *does not* look upon it as wrong. . . . He [Douglas] contends that whatever community wants slaves has a right to have them. So they have if it is not a wrong. But if it is a wrong, he cannot say people have a right to do wrong."

Lincoln persisted: ". . .That is the real issue. That is the issue that will continue in this country when these poor tongues of Judge Douglas and myself shall be silent. It is the eternal struggle between these two principles

"The Little Giant" was the nickname of eloquent, fiery Senator Stephen A. Douglas, who stood little more than five feet tall.

—right and wrong—throughout the world. They are the two principles that have stood face to face from the beginning of time; and will ever continue to struggle. The one is the common right of humanity and the other the divine right of kings. It is the same principle in whatever shape it develops itself. It is the same spirit that says, 'You work and toil and earn bread, and I'll eat it.' No matter in what shape it comes, whether from the mouth of a king who seeks to bestride the people of his own nation and live by the fruit of their labor, or from one race of men as an apology for enslaving another race, it is the same tyrannical principle."

On November 2, Illinois went to the polls. The popular vote for Republican representatives and senators exceeded the vote for Democrats by more than 4,000. But at that time senators were elected by state legislatures rather than the people at large. And because of an outdated apportionment of seats which favored the Democrats in southern Illinois, Douglas won a clear majority of votes in the legislature.

Lincoln accepted his defeat with good grace, remarking that it had been "a slip and not a fall." He plunged back into his law practice to make up for the time and money he had lost during the months of debates and speeches. Soon after, he hitched up his buggy and rode off on the Eighth Judicial Circuit, unmindful that his debates with Douglas had made him a figure of national importance.

This 1860 photograph is the only full length portrait of Lincoln who said of himself: "I am in height six feet four inches, nearly."

ILLINOIS STATE CAPITOL, PHOTOGRAPH BY HERBERT GEORG

The Lincoln-Douglas debates provided Illinois' summer excitement in 1858. In this painting Lincoln addresses a crowd at Charleston during the fourth debate. Douglas, at his right, listens thoughtfully and prepares an answer.

5

RAIL-SPLITTER CANDIDATE

One rainy night in 1858, as Lincoln and Henry Villard a young reporter from the *New York Staats-Zeitung* were waiting for a train that was late, Lincoln began musing about politics. He joked about his wife's fervent belief that he could become President. "Just think of such a sucker as me being President," said Lincoln with a laugh.

But since the Senate race against Douglas, a great many people had begun to think of Lincoln as a possible contender for the Presidency. In April of 1859 the editor of the *Rock Island* [Illinois] *Register* suggested that Lincoln might well be the next Republican presidential candidate. Lincoln stated with searching honesty, "I do not think myself fit for the Presidency."

Yet for all his humility, he could not deny that his nationally published debates with Douglas had spread his reputation far beyond the borders of Illinois. Men of intelligence and power had been impressed with Lincoln's clear, incisive thinking. Requests to speak came from Iowa, Indiana, New York, New Hampshire, Pennsylvania, and Ohio.

On September 30, 1859, Lincoln was in Milwaukee, Wisconsin, to give the principal address at the state fair. His speech was billed as nonpolitical, but Lincoln understood the free-soil spirit of the Wisconsin farmers, and his remarks had highly political overtones. He said the Southern "mudsill" theory of labor assumes that capital is all-important; that nobody labors unless he is induced to do it; and that labor and education are incompatible according to the old rule that educated people do not perform manual labor.

Contrasting the mudsill theory with free-soil thinking, Lincoln said that

This life-size poster of Lincoln, the rail-splitter candidate, was used in the presidential race of 1860. Shown as the ideal of Western vigor and virtue, Lincoln drives a wedge into a log as a vision of the distant White House calls him to higher duties.

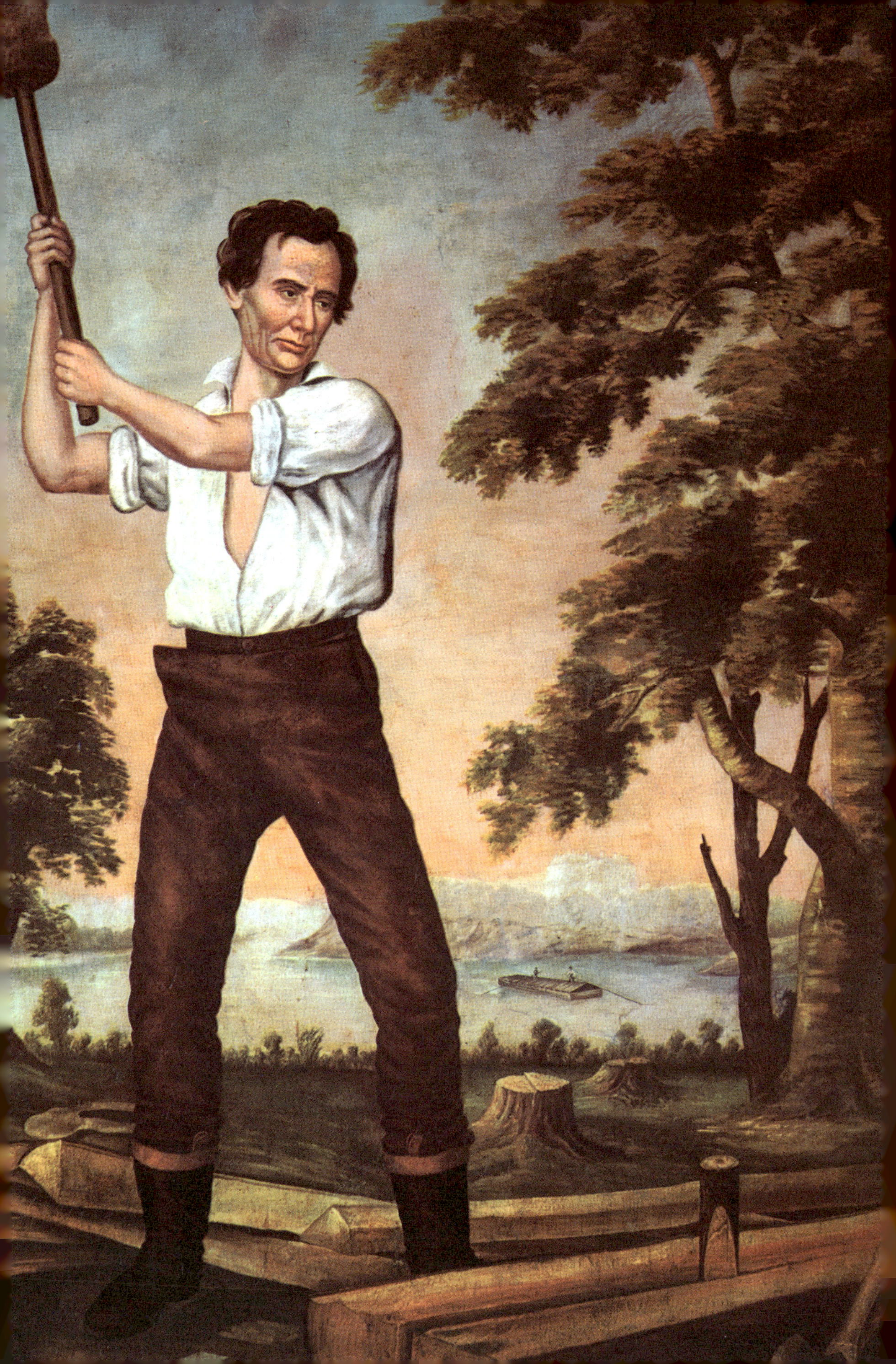

free-soilers held labor to be "prior to and independent of capital; that, in fact, capital is the fruit of labor." He remarked that, "*Now*, especially in these free states nearly all are educated. . . . It follows from this, that henceforth educated people must labour. . . . Free Labour insists on universal education."

The Wisconsin farmers applauded and cheered. They knew that Lincoln had been attacking the Southern states righters who had fought against the use of Congressional power to tax for the general welfare, and who had opposed the establishment of state universities.

Looking back at the success of his speaking engagements, even Lincoln began to think of himself as a possible presidential candidate. That December he made five speeches in Kansas and supplied his old friend Jesse W. Fell with material for a biographical sketch. This was to be published in Republican newspapers to make him better known in the East.

Lincoln wondered how much drawing power his name would have in the nominating convention, for it seemed highly probable that the Republicans would carry the election of 1860. The coalition of Northern compromisers and Southern die-hards that had kept the Democrats so long in power showed definite signs of crumbling.

But he was not the only Republican gazing hopefully at the stars as the bells rang out on New Year's Eve. In the first rank of Republican contenders was William H. Seward. He was a former governor of New York, and had been a United States senator since 1848. Seward was firmly on record against the extension of slavery. Even more radical than Seward was Salmon P. Chase, who had served two terms as governor of Ohio and one as a United States senator. There were still others—Edward Bates, a former antislavery congressman from Missouri; old Justice John McLean of Ohio, who was loved by abolitionists for his dissenting opinion in the Dred Scott Case; and the tricky, superpolitician Simon Cameron of Pennsylvania.

What chance had Lincoln against this crowd? The answer was that in early January Joseph Medill, editor of the *Chicago Tribune*, was in Washington talking of Lincoln's strength in terms of the weaknesses of the other candidates. On February 16, the *Tribune* came out with an emphatic endorsement of Lincoln as a presidential candidate.

Lincoln helped his own cause considerably by addressing a Republican club at Cooper Union in New York on the twenty-seventh of February. Dressed in a new, but travel-creased broadcloth suit, Lincoln appeared nervous as he faced a large audience representing "the intellect and moral culture" of the city. But as he launched into his argument, he rapidly gained confidence. First he examined the voting record of the original signers of the Constitution and the men who had passed the first ten amendments. This analysis offered conclusive proof that the Founding Fathers never "forbade the Federal Government to control slavery in the federal territories."

Next he defended the Republican party, saying that it could be labeled sectional only if Southerners wished to call it that. He referred to John Brown's raid on Harpers Ferry the previous October, saying that Republicans neither inspired it nor sanctioned it. Lincoln asked for peace. But he stated that if moral judgment made it necessary for Republicans to "stand by our duty, fearlessly and effectively," then, he said: "Neither let us be slandered from our duty by false accusations against us, nor frightened from it by menaces of destruction to the Government nor of dungeons to ourselves. *Let us have faith that right makes might, and in that faith let us, to the end, dare to do our duty as we understand it.*"

The crowd cheered wildly, and gave

Though strong in 1860, the Republicans had attracted many malcontents at first. This cartoon mocks Frémont's attempt to unify the party in 1856 by showing him promising everything to Negroes, Catholics, free love advocates, laborers, feminists, and teetotalers.

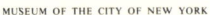

Lincoln's address at Cooper Union in New York in February of 1860 gained him the support of powerful and influential Republicans throughout the East. The painting above shows New York businessmen thronging Wall Street a few years earlier.

Lincoln a standing ovation. Men and women rushed to the platform to shake his hand. He had carried New York City by storm.

In triumph, Lincoln left the city to visit his son Robert who was studying at Phillips Exeter Academy in New Hampshire. Republican leaders in the towns along Lincoln's route requested him to speak, and his trip became a highly successful stump of New England.

By mid-March he was back in Springfield, happy with his achievements. A little more than a month later, writing Senator Lyman Trumbull of Illinois, he discussed his chances for the presidential nomination with complete frankness: "The taste *is* in my mouth a little."

In May it became apparent that the Democratic National Convention meeting in Charleston, South Carolina, was deadlocked over sectional differences. The party had split into a Northern faction supporting Douglas, and a Southern faction backing Vice President John C. Breckinridge of Kentucky. The field was fragmented even further by the formation of the Constitutional Union Party made up of old-line Whigs and disgruntled Know-Nothings. They had nominated John Bell of Tennessee on a platform supporting the Union and obedience to the Constitution.

As the Republican convention approached, Lincoln kept his hand well concealed. He believed that only the Illinois delegation would be unanimous for him at the outset. His instructions to one of his Ohio supporters were frank: "Our policy, then, is to give no offense to others—leave them in a mood to come to us, if they shall be impelled to give up their first love."

A week before the convention at Chicago, the Illinois Republicans met at Decatur for the purpose of endorsing Lincoln as their favorite son. John Hanks, Lincoln's aging cousin, stampeded the session by carrying in two fence rails with a banner reading: "ABRAHAM LINCOLN, *The Rail Candidate for President in 1860*: Two Rails from a Lot of 3,000 made in 1830 by Thos. Hanks and Abe Lincoln—Whose Father was the First Pioneer of Macon County."

Lincoln remained in Springfield when the Illinois delegation left for Chicago. Murat Halstead, a reporter from Cincinnati, quickly sensed the mood of the convention. He wrote that even before the balloting began, the movements for Bates, McLean, Cameron, and Chase had "gone down like lead in the mighty waters." The candidate would be either Seward or Lincoln.

For the first two days, the convention struggled to agree on a platform that would appeal to all the dissident groups in the party. Among the many planks adopted the most important concerned the issue of slavery: the Republicans denied the existence of any legal right to extend slavery into the territories.

Since the first day in Chicago the supporters of the two hopefuls had been busy cajoling votes and making promises. Lincoln had repeatedly warned his managers not to commit him to any deals. He sent them a telegram to that effect just as they sat down to bargain with two of Cameron's henchmen for the decisive Pennsylvania votes. But Judge David Davis, his campaign manager, muttered "Lincoln ain't here." Davis won the needed votes by promising Cameron a Cabinet post.

The first ballot gave $173\frac{1}{2}$ votes to Seward and 102 to Lincoln—233 were necessary for the nomination. On the second ballot New Hampshire was the first delegation to switch votes to Lincoln. "A blighting blow upon the Seward interest," Halstead reported. By the time the tally was announced, Seward had $184\frac{1}{2}$ votes, but Lincoln had climbed to 181! The trend was now clear. The third ballot carried the nomination for Lincoln. Jubilant over their victory, Lincoln's floor managers wired Springfield: "We did it. Glory to God!"

Springfield erupted into near-delirium when Lincoln's nomination was finally confirmed. Lincoln, perhaps the calmest man in town, had read the telegram in the newspaper office. It was soon jammed with people who had come to shake his hand and cheer his success. Eyes twinkling, Lincoln announced: "Gentlemen, you had better come up and shake my hand while you can; honors elevate some men, you know." Then his mood sobered. "Well, gentlemen," he said, "there is a little short woman at our house who is probably more interested in this dispatch than I am; and, if you will excuse me, I will take it up and let her see it."

It was unheard of in those days for a candidate to campaign for himself. This was done by members of the party who stumped the country in his behalf. So Lincoln stayed in Springfield—keeping close watch on events.

Douglas, however, feeling that he was the only candidate who could beat Lincoln and save the Union, ignored the tradition. In spite of illness he set out on a whirlwind campaign to win the free states. When early state elections in the North showed heavy Republican majorities, Douglas stumped the Southern states. But just as the North considered him proslavery, the South thought him too antislavery.

The election was itself almost an anticlimax. The Democratic split was too wide to defeat the Republicans. Lincoln polled a popular majority of nearly 500,000 votes over Douglas, his nearest competitor, and secured a solid majority of the electoral votes.

The news of Lincoln's election increased secessionist turmoil in the

OFF AND RUNNING

Chicago hastily put up the Wigwam (left) to house the 1860 Republican convention. Lincoln's managers packed the house with boosters and gained him the nomination. The cartoon below shows long-legged Abe, "The Fittest of all Candidates," outdistancing all the other contenders.

South. There was widespread fear of a slave revolt. And there had also been a severe drought. A bad cotton crop would ruin many Southern planters who were heavily in debt to Northern financiers. Such economic disaster could destroy Southern political power forever. The previous October Governor William H. Gist of South Carolina had taken a secret poll of the other Southern governors to see if their states were willing to secede should Lincoln be elected. At least half of them replied that while they were not willing to be the first to secede, they would be willing to follow the lead of another Southern state.

In the anxious weeks between the November election and the March inauguration, Buchanan's government was faced with the impossible task of holding the Union together. On December 18, 1860, the Senate formed the Committee of Thirteen to find a way to quiet Southern fears. John J. Crittenden of Kentucky led the peacemaking effort by proposing amendments to the Constitution which would guarantee noninterference with the institution of slavery and the slave trade. He also proposed the extension of the Missouri Compromise line to

81

The 1860 Republican campaign poster above shows Lincoln and Hannibal Hamlin of Maine. Their platform opposed the extension of slavery, but proclaimed "The Union must and shall be preserved." Though Lincoln stayed in Springfield, the campaign came to him. At the rally at his home below, he is the tall figure in white at the right of the door.

California—prohibiting slavery north of 36°30′, and recognizing it to the south of that line.

But hotheaded secessionist leaders were in no mood to compromise. On December 20, South Carolina took the first step. By a unanimous vote in convention, the state seceded from the Union.

Senator Seward, the leading Republican on the Committee of Thirteen, believed that the Crittenden Compromise could still save the Union. Before voting, Seward asked the President-elect, who had just offered him the post of Secretary of State, for his opinion on the issue.

On December 22 Lincoln's position was made clear—"Let there be no compromise on the question of extending slavery." On this point he stated, "I am inflexible." However he did not object to Crittenden's other proposals. In private talks in Springfield, Lincoln was doing his best to calm the fears of Southern leaders.

But the passage of the compromise depended on the crucial Republican votes. When Seward voted against the extension of the Missouri Compromise line, Crittenden's proposal failed. Even if it had passed, it is doubtful that the Union could have been saved. After South Carolina's decision was announced, secessionist conventions swept through the South. By the first day of February Mississippi, Florida, Alabama, Georgia, Louisiana, and Texas had brought to seven the number of states in the "house divided."

Against the background of these ominous events, Lincoln found himself caught up in the whirlwind of activity that surrounds a newly-elected President. He was besieged with visitors, newsmen, office-seekers, anxious Northern and Southern leaders, and Cabinet hopefuls. His home and office were deluged with mail, including many poisonous letters maligning him personally, some even threatening his life.

Still, Lincoln managed to slip away every now and then to work on the first draft of his inaugural address. And he made time for a visit to Coles County to say goodbye to his beloved stepmother. Some people claim Sarah Bush Lincoln cried out, "Abe, I'll never see you alive again. They'll kill you." Lincoln gave a laugh and said quietly, "Don't worry. Everything will come out all right."

On February 6 the Lincolns held a farewell reception for their Springfield friends, but for the President-elect one important act remained. Alone he called on Billy Herndon in the offices they had shared for sixteen years. Herndon later wrote that Lincoln "recalled some incidents of his early practice and took great pleasure in delineating the ludicrous features of many a lawsuit on the circuit."

As the two partners walked down the stairs, Lincoln glanced at their old sign—Lincoln & Herndon—which swung on its rusty hinges at the foot of the stairway. "Let it hang there undisturbed," he told Billy. Then his

This charming view of the south front of the White House was painted by an English visitor, L. G. Cranston, in 1860. The only room that is preserved today with furnishings and décor as they were in that period is the Lincoln Suite which lies behind the corner windows on the right side of the second floor.

cheerful mood seemed to slip away. After a time Herndon heard him mutter: "I am sick of office-holding already, and I shudder when I think of the tasks that are still ahead."

A drizzling rain fell on the Great Western station on the morning of February 11. Mrs. Lincoln and the boys, planning to leave a few days later, joined the throng of more than a thousand fellow-townsmen who had come to bid Lincoln good-by. For twenty minutes he stood in the waiting room, shaking hands. No one could doubt his deep emotion. His face looked pale. He could hardly speak. Presently he mounted the rear platform of the train, looking down into the faces of his devoted neighbors. "I now leave," he said, "not knowing when, or whether ever, I may return, with a task before me greater than that which rested upon Washington.... Trusting in Him who can go with me, and remain with you, and be everywhere for good, let us confidently hope that all will yet be well. To His care commending you, as I hope in your prayers you will commend me, I bid you an affectionate farewell."

They stood watching, in the rain, as the train bore Lincoln away.

6

THE THREAT OF WAR

There were lively times in Montgomery, Alabama, that February of 1861. Into this city, set like Rome on seven hills, came delegates from the seven Southern states that had broken with the Union. Within two weeks they formed a new government, framed a constitution, and inaugurated Jefferson Davis of Mississippi as provisional president of the Confederate States of America. Except for Fort Sumter in Charlestown Harbor, forts Jefferson and Pickens in Pensacola Bay, and two small forts off the Florida coast, all Federal forts, arsenals, customhouses, and lighthouses in the Confederacy were now in Southern hands. The Post Office Department continued to function until June, but only because Southerners found using the mails convenient.

These rapidly unfolding events made Lincoln's journey to Washington an exhausting ordeal. Instead of the normal two or three days, the trip was lengthened to twelve to allow as many people as possible to see and hear the new President. Disturbed and anxious at the news from the South, crowds gathered at every town and city along the route to judge what kind of man Lincoln might be, and to hope for reassuring words from him.

In Indianapolis, and Cincinnati, and Pittsburgh, he spoke with cautious, considered words. He made no fiery declarations or glib promises. People seemed disappointed and unsatisfied.

At Westfield, New York, Lincoln spoke to little Grace Bedell who had written him suggesting that he might look more dignified if he grew a beard. After speaking in Buffalo, where ten thousand people turned out to stare at the man from the West, Lincoln journeyed on to Albany. Arriving in New York City on February 20, Lincoln had to cope with yet another round of exhausting ceremonies, and had to address crowds that seemed only lukewarm. That night he attended his first opera and wore black gloves

B. & O. RAILROAD MUSEUM

Because of threats to his life, Lincoln arrived unannounced in Washington. With his guards close behind, he was escorted from the station by Illinois congressman Elihu Washburne.

Crossing Baltimore secretly at night on the advice of fearful friends, Lincoln (tallest man in picture above) reached Camden station safely.

instead of white. The hostile press ridiculed him severely for this breach of etiquette.

On the twenty-first Lincoln had to face the people of New Jersey, who voted against him in the recent election. But they welcomed him warmly. As he addressed the State Assembly Lincoln revealed his true attitude toward the secessionists: "I shall do all that may be in my power to promote a peaceful settlement of all our difficulties. The man does not live who is more devoted to peace than I am. . . . But it may be necessary to put the foot down firmly." The *New York Tribune* reported: "Here the audience broke out into cheers so loud and long that for some moments it was impossible to hear Mr. L's voice."

Distressing news awaited Lincoln when he arrived in Philadelphia that afternoon. The Pinkerton detective agency reported that their agents had uncovered a plot to assassinate Lincoln as he changed trains at Baltimore. The President-elect was urged to leave for Washington that very night. "This he flatly refused to do," wrote one of Lincoln's advisors. "He had engagements with the people, he said, to raise a flag over Independence Hall in the morning, and to exhibit himself at Harrisburg in the afternoon—and

88

these engagements he would not break in any event."

Lincoln was well aware of the dangers of his position, but he remained calm and showed no alarm. The precautions taken for his safety annoyed him for he felt it necessary "that the people know I come among them without fear." But later that night the son of William Seward, Lincoln's future Secretary of State, brought an urgent letter from a totally new informant describing the same assassination plot.

With this proof before him, Lincoln grudgingly agreed to travel by an unscheduled train to Washington after his Harrisburg engagement. He reached the capital at six o'clock on the chilly morning of February 23. He was met by an old friend and escorted to temporary quarters at Willard's Hotel.

Despite the early morning arrival, the President-elect quickly displayed a cheerful mood. He breakfasted at Willard's with Seward, and the two men paid a call at the Executive Mansion. President Buchanan, who was conducting a Cabinet meeting at the time, was greatly surprised when the doorman presented Lincoln's card. "Uncle Abe is downstairs!" he cried, and rushed out to greet him.

Later, in Parlor Number 6 at Willard's, Lincoln received the delegates from 21 states who had gathered at a last-ditch Peace Conference to try to salvage the Union. During the conversation one Southern delegate told Lincoln, "Everything now depends upon you." He replied, "I cannot

Lincoln was ridiculed by cartoonists for supposedly traveling to Washington disguised in an army cloak and a scotch cap.

89

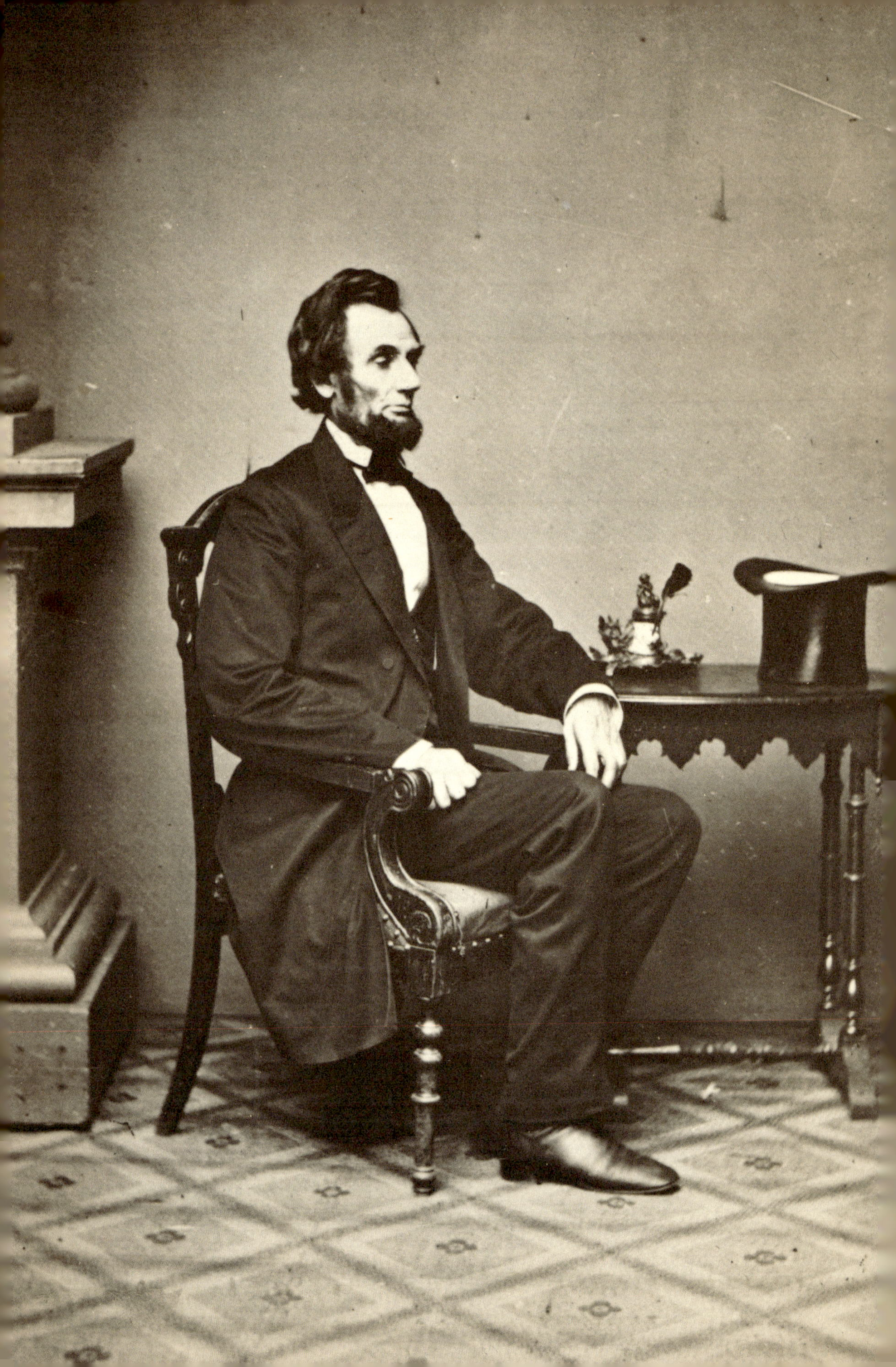

agree to that. My course is as plain as a turnpike road. It is marked out by the Constitution. I am in no doubt which way to go. Suppose now we all stop discussing and try the experiment of obedience to the Constitution and the laws. Don't you think it would work?"

No one attending the Peace Conference answered that question unequivocally except Lincoln. He believed with all his heart that the Union must survive and told the delegates, "If I shall ever come to the great office of President . . . I shall swear that I will faithfully execute the office of President . . . of all the United States, and that I will, to the best of my ability, preserve, protect, and defend the Constitution. . . . [which] will not be preserved until it is enforced and obeyed in every part of every one of the United States."

On March 4, 1861, Lincoln donned a new suit for his inaugural. Riding beside Buchanan on the way to the ceremony, he appeared completely at ease. Yet Pennsylvania Avenue rooftops, street intersections, and the Capitol grounds were being closely guarded by Federal soldiers, cavalrymen, and artillery. But if Lincoln knew that two Union riflemen lurked behind each window where the wings of the Capitol flanked the inaugural stand, he gave no indication of that fact as he addressed the throng before him.

He spoke simply and temperately, arguing against the right of secession.

SALMON P. CHASE
Secretary of the Treasury

EDWIN M. STANTON
Secretary of War

WILLIAM H. SEWARD
Secretary of State

MINISTERS AND RIVALS

Despite their intense rivalry, Lincoln wanted the capable services of Salmon P. Chase and William H. Seward in his Cabinet. Made Secretary of State, Seward thought little of Lincoln's ability and sent him a memo on how to run the country. Lincoln replied emphatically that he and only he must direct policy. Seward curbed his ambition and became the President's trusted advisor. But Chase, who became Secretary of the Treasury, felt he was better qualified than Lincoln to run the country. His bid for the 1864 presidential nomination cost him his Cabinet post. When Edwin Stanton became Secretary of War in 1862 he argued violently with Lincoln. Yet at times he seemed the only man who shared the President's passion to save the Union by winning the war.

The famous photographer Mathew Brady made this portrait of Lincoln the day the President-elect arrived in Washington.

In a calm voice Lincoln stated that his government would "hold, occupy and possess the property and places belonging to the government." But he voiced no intention to repossess that property already seized by Southern insurgents.

He concluded with a magnificent paragraph: "I am loth to close. We are not enemies, but friends. We must not be enemies. Though passion may have strained, it must not break our bonds of affection. The mystic chords of memory, stretching from every battlefield, and patriot grave, to every living heart and hearthstone, all over this broad land, will yet swell the chorus of the Union, when again touched, as surely they will be, by the better angels of our nature."

Old Chief Justice Taney—looking, one witness said, like "a galvanized corpse"—administered the oath of office that made Lincoln the sixteenth President of the United States.

If at the inaugural ball that evening Lincoln appeared to be "a long, awkward figure," his abstraction did not surprise those on the inside of the government. There were serious difficulties within the new administration. Seward was convinced that Lincoln intended to permit Salmon P. Chase of Ohio to become the dominant figure in the Cabinet, and had threatened to resign. But Lincoln managed to soothe this flight of peevishness and Seward remained.

The next day, however, there was a deeper crisis to be considered. At the time that South Carolina seceded, the only fort occupied by Federal troops had been Moultrie, a broken-down work that could never be defended successfully. But Major Robert Anderson, who commanded Moultrie, did not allow his personal sentiments as a native Kentuckian to interfere with his higher duties as a Federal officer.

Across from Fort Moultrie, in mid-harbor where it governed every entrance and exit by water to Charleston, stood Fort Sumter. Without warning on the day after Christmas, 1860, Anderson occupied Sumter. The presence of Federal troops in the fort angered the secessionists. They felt that Anderson's move had been an act of open aggression against the Confederacy. In the North, Fort Sumter became the symbol of the Union and of Federal authority. On March 5, the day after Lincoln had been inaugurated, South Carolina refused Anderson the right to purchase supplies. The major sent Lincoln a dispatch warning that without new supplies of food he could not hold out beyond April 15.

In the days following, army leaders stated that Sumter could never be held. With equal vigor navy leaders expressed the opposite view. Lincoln, caught in the middle, hesitated. He remembered the children of Israel on the shore of the Red Sea. "Stand still and see the salvation of the Lord," Moses had said. The President believed that he had time to wait.

In Montgomery, Alabama, Jefferson Davis chafed as he tried to guess

The empty shell of the unfinished Capitol dome loomed over the dignitaries and crowds of people who had come to hear the inaugural address of Abraham Lincoln on March 4, 1861.

what kind of game Lincoln was playing. From Washington came one clue: the national government appeared to believe that "secession movements were short-lived" and that they tended to "wither under sunshine." Certainly Mr. Lincoln realized how valuable an ally he could make of time—time for the moderates to beat down the fire-eaters in Virginia's continuing secession convention; time for ascertaining the true situation in Charleston and Fort Sumter; time for giving unionists the opportunity to win the upper hand in the key border states.

Yet Lincoln could not allow Major Anderson and his small garrison to be starved into the surrender of Sumter, and he ordered provisions (but no reinforcements) sent to the fort. He notified the governor of South Carolina of his intentions on April 8. This meant that the Federal troops would remain at Sumter, and the Confederates in Charleston grew impatient. Under the command of the dapper little Creole, Brigadier General P. G. T. Beauregard, the city bristled with war preparations.

On the eleventh of April Beauregard sent Anderson a note demanding the surrender of the fort. Anderson replied, "My sense of honor, and of my obligations to my Government, prevent my compliance." But he remarked to Beauregard's messengers, "If you do not batter us to pieces, we shall be starved out in a few days."

However South Carolina and the Confederate government felt they had

Two months after the Mercury *announced South Carolina's secession (right), Jefferson Davis was sworn in as President of the Confederacy (above).*

CHARLESTON MERCURY

EXTRA:

Passed unanimously at 1.15 o'clock, P. M., December 20th, 1860.

AN ORDINANCE

To dissolve the Union between the State of South Carolina and other States united with her under the compact entitled " The Constitution of the United States of America."

We, the People of the State of South Carolina, in Convention assembled, do declare and ordain, and it is hereby declared and ordained,

That the Ordinance adopted by us in Convention, on the twenty-third day of May, in the year of our Lord one thousand seven hundred and eighty-eight, whereby the Constitution of the United States of America was ratified, and also, all Acts and parts of Acts of the General Assembly of this State, ratifying amendments of the said Constitution, are hereby repealed; and that the union now subsisting between South Carolina and other States, under the name of "The United States of America," is hereby dissolved.

THE UNION IS DISSOLVED!

been put off long enough. At 4:30 on the morning of April 12, 1861, Beauregard ordered the battle to begin. Across Charleston Harbor came a flash of light and the dull roar of a mortar.

From the moment the first bulletins were posted of the firing on Sumter, all business stopped in the North. Men gathered around newspaper offices, grimly silent at first. Then they began to vent their increasing anger with shouts of "Avenge the insult!" and "Vindicate the nation's honor!"

When Lincoln heard of the bombardment and subsequent capture of Sumter he remained calm. But he vented his anger in his July 4 message to Congress. "They knew that this government desired to keep the garrison in the fort, not to assail them, but merely to maintain visible possession, and thus to preserve the Union from actual and immediate dissolution—trusting . . . to the ballot box for final adjustment. . . . They assailed and reduced the fort for precisely the reverse object."

On Sunday, April 14, Stephen A.

MAJOR ROBERT ANDERSON GENERAL P.G.T. BEAUREGARD

The Civil War began on April 12, 1861, when, after polite negotiations, Brigadier General P.G.T. Beauregard opened fire on the sixty-five man garrison at Fort Sumter in the Charleston Harbor commanded by his former artillery instructor, Major Robert Anderson. Beauregard's well-positioned cannon (left) battered for thirty-seven hours at the fort's walls with such effect that, with barracks afire and men exhausted, there was no choice for Anderson but capitulation.

Douglas called on Lincoln. Not as rivals, but as fellow statesmen, they discussed the crisis. Lincoln showed Douglas the proclamation he intended issuing next day calling for 75,000 volunteers to serve the nation for the next three months.

"Mr. President," Douglas said, "I cordially concur in every word of that document, except that instead of a call for 75,000 men I would make it 200,000. You do not know the dishonest purposes of those men [the Confederates] as well as I do." Walking to a wall map, Douglas pointed to strategic points that should be immediately strengthened—Fort Monroe in Virginia, Harpers Ferry on the Potomac, Cairo on the Mississippi, and Washington. In Lincoln he found "an earnest and gratified listener."

As the North had misjudged the strength of secessionist feeling, so the Confederacy had underestimated the North's determination to stand by the Union. Volunteers rushed to enlist and Horace Greeley believed that 500,000 men would have responded

COOK COLLECTION, VALENTINE MUSEUM

The country-bred boys who joined the Confederate army after Sumter knew how to handle firearms. These newly-outfitted volunteers tried to look martial for the photographer.

had Lincoln asked for them. On the seventeenth the state of Virginia, undecided for some time which way to go, seceded from the Union. Confederate troops were given immediate permission to enter the state, and the Virginia militia was ordered to capture the Federal arsenal at Harpers Ferry.

Learning of the Southern move, the Union guards set fire to arms and ammunition worth millions of dollars, and evacuated the fort. Two days later the commander of the Union Navy Yard at Norfolk, thinking he was under attack, ordered the Yard set afire and evacuated his men; an additional thirty million dollars worth of Federal property went up in flames.

Stephen Douglas, who had warned against some such maneuver, threw himself into a barnstorming journey through parts of western Virginia, and into Ohio and Illinois to rally support to the Union. In Chicago Douglas spoke to a huge crowd saying, "Before God it is the duty of every American citizen to rally around the flag of his country." It was his last speech. Exhausted by this final effort for his country, the ailing Douglas died on the third of June.

When Virginia announced secession, her renowned soldier, General Robert E. Lee, faced a difficult decision. On April 18 he was called to Washington and offered command of the main Federal army in the field. Lee said afterward: "I declined the offer . . . stating as candidly and as courteously as I could that, though opposed to secession and deprecating war, I could take no part in an invasion of the Southern states."

The first Union regiment to start for Washington in answer to Lincoln's call was the Sixth Massachusetts. As the soldiers were changing trains in Baltimore on April 19, they were attacked by Southern partisans. Four enlisted men and twelve civilians were killed in the bloody riot that followed.

At five o'clock the weary Massachusetts troops reached a shocked national capital and took up quarters in the Senate Chamber. After the riot, troops en route to Washington were shunted around Baltimore, slowing their progress several days. With telegraph lines cut, the capital was isolated, despairing, filled with gloomy apprehension.

Southern papers had been screaming for the capture of Washington, and the flickering of Confederate campfires could be seen across the Potomac at night. Sentinels stood at attention before the entrances to the White House and governmental departments. A note of cheer in the Executive Mansion was the arrival of the mail from New York City—three days late. Newspapers told of the departure of the Seventh Regiment for Washington; of a gigantic meeting of Northern sympathizers in Union Square; of wild, jubilant patriotism everywhere.

But day after day the troops did not arrive. Lincoln could no longer dis-

MICHIGAN HISTORICAL COLLECTIONS, UNIVERSITY OF MICHIGAN

RALLY ROUND

THE UNION FOREVER

THE FLAG, BOYS!

100 MEN WANTED!!

For the 23d Mich. Infantry.

Enlist before April 1st, secure the Government Bounty of $300 00,

AND "KEEP OUT OF THE DRAFT!"

Government Bounty, $300; State Bounty, $100; Town Bounty, $100.
Apply to WM. SICKELS, St. Johns, or

O. L. SPAULDING,

Lieut. Col., 23d Mich. Infantry, Corunna.
March , 1864.

("REPUBLICAN" PRINT, ST. JOHNS.)

This poster used patriotic slogans to urge Michigan boys to sign up, but the clincher was: "Keep out of the draft!" Lincoln's unpopular draft act was passed in March, 1863.

guise his anxiety, and one day standing by a window, gazing wistfully at the Potomac, he cried: "Why don't they come! Why don't they come!"

Then on April 25, a Thursday, the soldiers of the Seventh New York began arriving on railroad cars at the Washington depot. John Nicolay and John Hay, Lincoln's private secretaries, never forgot the proud sight of those men marching up Pennsylvania Avenue to the White House: "As they passed up the magnificent street, with their well-formed ranks, their exact military step, their soldierly bearing, their gayly floating flags, and the inspiring music of their splendid regimental band, they seemed to sweep all thought of danger and all taint of treason out of that great national thoroughfare and out of every human heart in the Federal city. . . . Cheer upon cheer greeted them; windows were thrown up; houses opened; the population came forth upon the streets as for a holiday. . . . For the first time, the combined spirit and power of liberty entered the nation's Capital."

After the arrival of the Seventh New York other troops began to arrive on schedule. But for Lincoln the bitter problems of war between the states were just beginning. State officials in Arkansas, North Carolina, and Tennessee did not wait for ordinances of secession to side with the Confederacy.

Yet there was good news, too. In June, by a popular vote of 92,460 to 37,700, the critical border state of Kentucky elected nine Union congressmen and only one secessionist. By the end of April Lincoln increased the Regular Army by ten regiments (22,714 men). He called for 42,000 three-year volunteers, and increased the Navy to 25,000.

A delight to Lincoln in these grim Washington days was Colonel Elmer E. Ellsworth whose finely trained, red-trousered Zouaves were a city attraction. For a time Ellsworth had been a student in Lincoln's law office. And the dashing young colonel was so close to the Lincoln family that he had caught the measles from Willie and Tad. During a maneuver on May 24 to capture the city and garrison of Alexandria, Virginia, the brave and daring Zouave tore down a Confederate flag that had taunted the capital across the river. As Ellsworth was leaving the hotel where the flag had flown, he was shot and killed. The tragedy of war stabbed straight into Lincoln's heart. Ellsworth's funeral was held at the White House.

Ellsworth dead—eleven days later, Douglas dead in Chicago: Lincoln was learning that he must live with the shocks of war in a North clamoring for a quick victory. Horace Greeley's newspaper proclaimed that the

Northern volunteers rushed to sign up to defend the Union. The print (above right) shows throngs around a placarded recruiting station in New York. But between Union marshaling points and Lincoln's beleaguered Washington lay Baltimore, where Southern sympathizers (below right) violently attacked the Sixth Massachusetts Regiment.

30,000 VOLUNTEERS WANTED
COUNTY BOUNTY CASH DOWN $ 300
STATE BOUNTY " 75
U.S. BOUNTY FOR NEW RECRUITS " 302
TOTAL TO NEW RECRUITS $ 677
U.S. BOUNTY TO VETERAN SOLDIERS EXTRA 100
TOTAL TO VETERAN SOLDIERS " 777
$ 15.00
HAND MONEY
Paid any Party who brings a
RECRUIT
HUBBEL & CO'S
GOLDEN BITTERS
G. 1863 B
BEST TONIC
IN THE
WORLD
CENTRAL DEPOT
AMERICAN EXPRESS
BUILDING
NEW YORK
A FINE WATCH FREE
AND 100 LARGE SIZE PRIZE
PACKAGES FOR $ 15
AGENTS WANTED.
S. C. RICKARDS & CO
182 NASSAU ST. N.Y.
A HANDSOME WATCH FOR ONLY
BRITTISH OFFICERS WATCHES ONLY
CHAS. P. MORTON & CO
40 ANN ST. N.Y
PIONEER BADGE MANUFACT
ALL KINDS OF ARMY BADGES IN
BY THE SINGLE ONE 100, OR 1000 & SENT
DROWNE & MOO
208 BROADWAY

The panic of troops, teamsters, and civilians at the First Battle of Bull Run is captured in this contemporary sketch.

"Rebel Congress" must not be allowed to meet on the twentieth of July in Richmond, now the capital of the Confederacy. Greeley sounded the battle cry, "Onward to Richmond!"

Lincoln had to make a quick move or lose public confidence. His military advice from General Winfield Scott, the aging chief of the Army, or from Brigadier General Irvin McDowell, commanding Federal forces in the field south of the Potomac, was for delay and preparation. But politics won, and a forward movement was ordered. On the banks of a stream called Bull Run, at Manassas Junction, Virginia, the first great battle of the war occurred on July 21, 1861.

That Sunday was grimly eventful for Lincoln. By noon the War Department had learned little except that the battle had started. In midafternoon a jittery President walked over to Scott's office and found the old general napping. Awakened, Scott told the President that not a thing could be made of early battle reports and that, really, he would like to continue his nap. Late afternoon brought a report of an obvious Union victory and Lincoln ordered his carriage for his usual evening's drive. When he returned, half an hour later, panic surrounded him. Southern reserves thrown into the battle had reversed the decision and now a telegram said: "General McDowell's army in full retreat through Centreville. The day is lost."

Bull Run was only some thirty miles southwest of Washington. Sight-seers had gone out to picnic near the battleground to watch the fray. Untrained troops, following orders, attempted the tricky maneuver of retreat in ranks. But they quickly ran into the civilians who had been terrified by the retreat, and had jammed the roads with their carriages. Cries of "The Rebels are coming!" turned what had begun as an orderly withdrawal into headlong panic.

At two o'clock on the morning of July 22, General Scott arrived at the White House to insist that Mrs. Lincoln and the boys leave for the north so that they would be out of danger. Mary Lincoln refused. The Lincolns had left Springfield as a family, she said, and only as a family would they depart from Washington.

In the gray, dismal dawn of Monday, the first fugitives from the defeat reached Washington. A drizzling rain fell on panic-stricken soldiers who wandered footsore and exhausted through the city's streets. But by noon it was clear that the Confederates were not following up their victory—Washington was safe.

So the North had fought and lost and would have to fight again in a conflict that threatened to become very long and very costly. Lincoln realized that he must accept that tragic truth. The next day he went out to visit the camps and forts surrounding Arlington Heights, Virginia. As he passed among the Union soldiers he spoke words of cheer and confidence.

Eager to show appreciation of Union soldiers, Lincoln often startled the men by coming up to shake hands and talk with them.

OVERLEAF: *Rank upon rank, the proud Army of the Potomac marches down Washington's Pennsylvania Avenue in 1861, led by the daring Zouaves in their colorful uniforms.*

COLLECTION OF ALEXANDER MCCOOK CRAIGHEAD

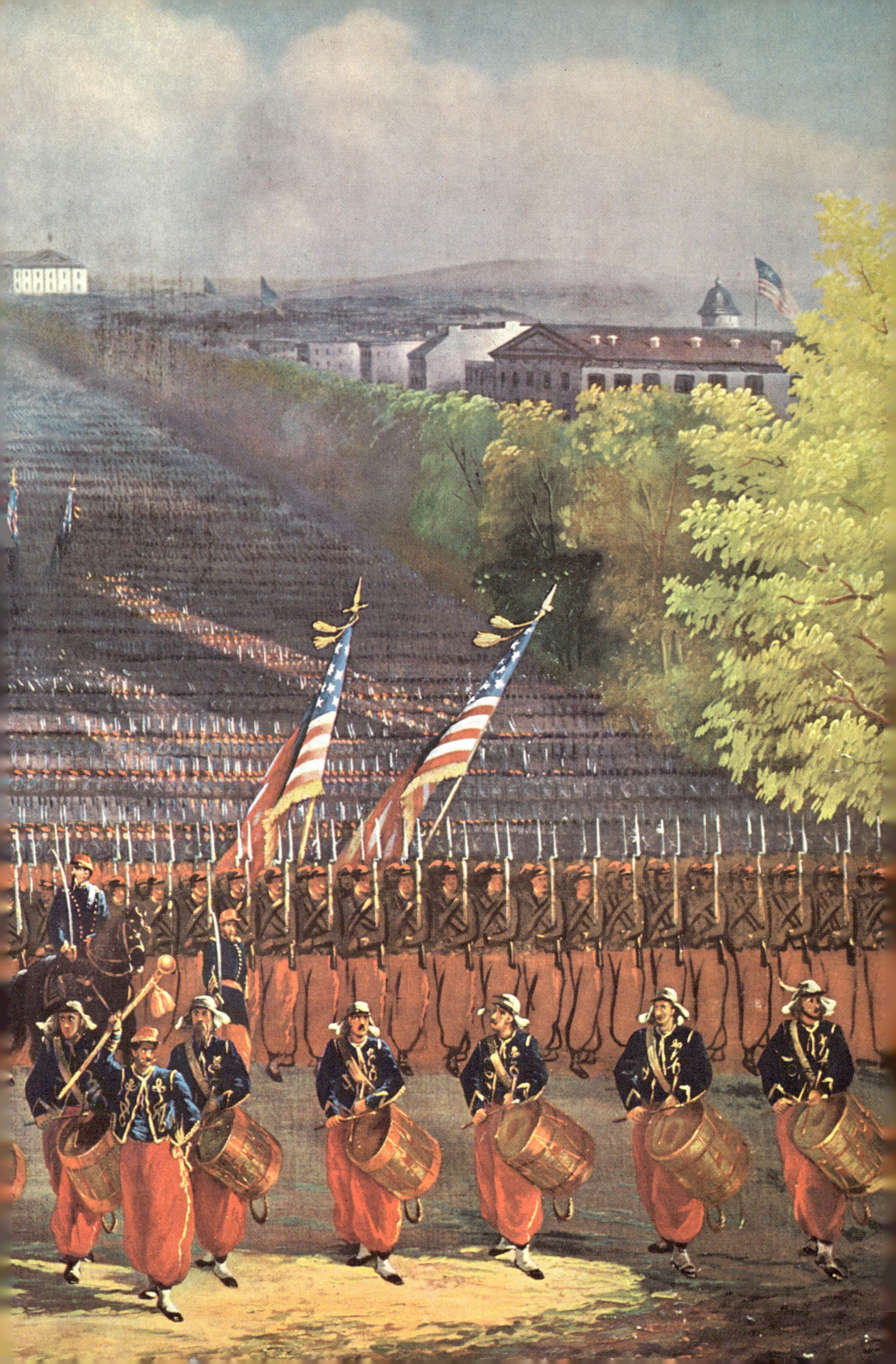

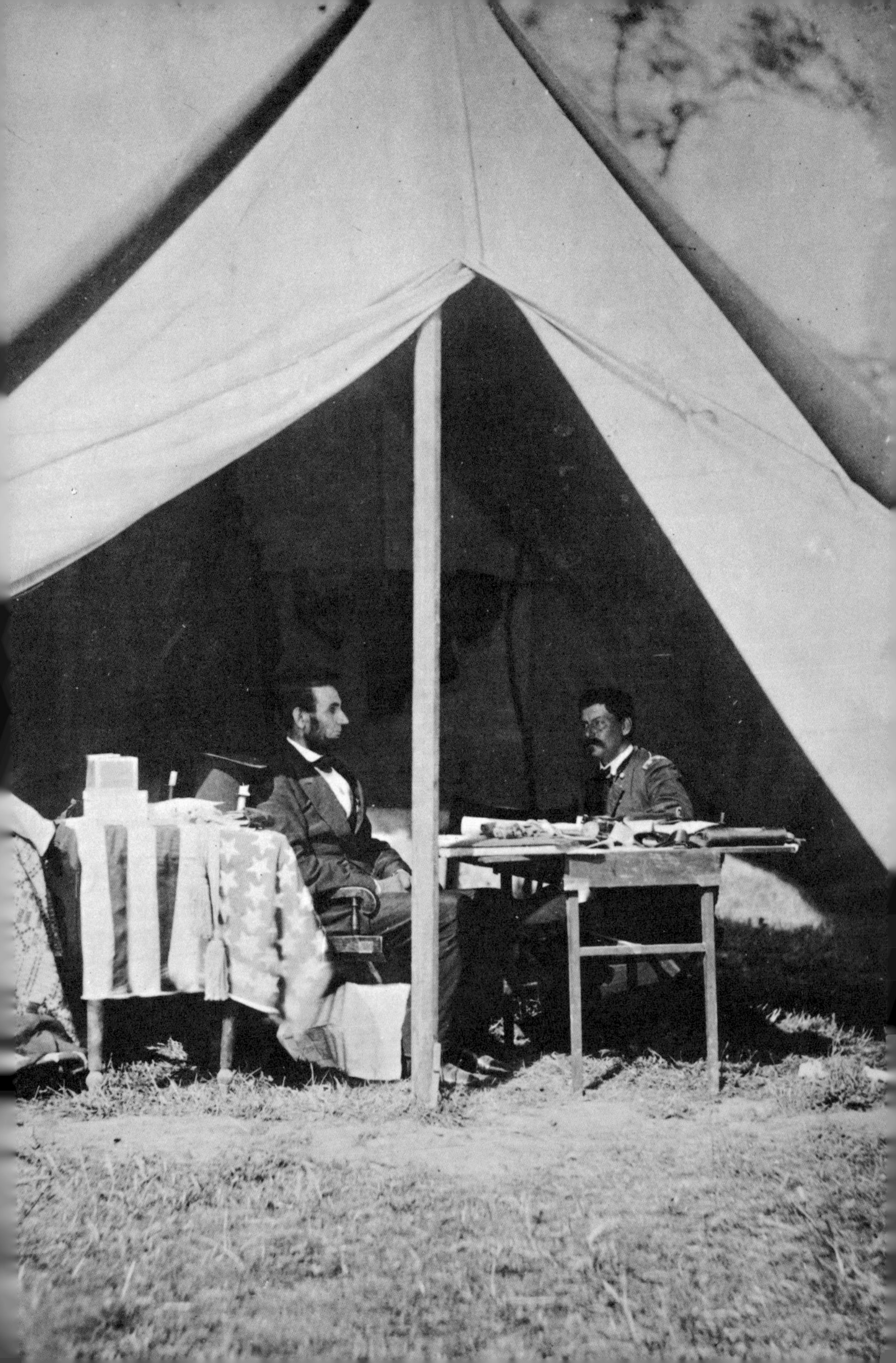

7

LINCOLN IS "WHIPPED AGAIN"

After the Battle of Bull Run the Union army was totally dispirited and disorganized. To give his forces some direction, Lincoln drew up a memorandum on future military policy. He stated that the Union "would hold present positions, tighten the blockade, replace the three-months volunteers with men enrolled for longer service, and then push expeditions simultaneously into Virginia . . . east Tennessee, and down the Mississippi."

The army and the nation responded to his call. But Lincoln still had to live with the responsibility of finding a general who could win a decisive battle. He faced pressure for military successes at home, and the real probability that England or France might recognize the Confederacy and intervene on its behalf.

Through a most ably contrived campaign General George Brinton McClellan had just managed to drive Confederate forces out of western Virginia, and had secured the area for the Union. Lincoln decided to pin his hopes on McClellan. Short, wiry, and red-headed, "Little Mac" was then thirty-five. After graduating from West Point in 1846, he had fought well in the Mexican War. In 1857 he had left the army to become a highly successful businessman.

When the war began, McClellan resigned his position to become a major general of the Ohio volunteers. Shortly after, he was commissioned in the Regular Army and was put in charge of the Department of the Ohio. This command led to McClellan's success in Virginia and a presidential appointment to head the Army of the Potomac.

In Washington, McClellan believed that he had found his real opportunity. The War Department was in chaos, and his administrative genius won the day. A superb organizer and discipli-

Framed by the open flaps of an army field tent, Lincoln sits with General McClellan who the President hoped would win the war for the Union. Mr. Lincoln's hat rests upon a camp table draped with an American flag.

107

narian, McClellan gave the demoralized Union army form, competence, and *esprit de corps.*

A vain man who had an exalted opinion of himself, McClellan wrote to his wife saying, "I find myself in a new and strange position here: President, cabinet, Gen. Scott, and all deferring to me. By some strange operation of magic I seem to have become the power of the land."

McClellan had other weaknesses: always believing that the enemy outnumbered him, he was hesitant to fight in the field. So he built elaborate defenses around Washington, and all during the summer and into the fall he drilled and paraded his men. He felt continually thwarted by Washing-

General Winfield Scott, victorious in the Mexican War (left), was too old for command in the Civil War. He stepped aside for General G. B. McClellan (right), seen leading troops out of camp in the painting above.

ton politics, and was openly contemptuous of the government—particularly of General Scott and the President.

But late in October Scott retired, opening the way for McClellan to become the President's general in chief. Yet full authority still did not prod McClellan into action, and a storm of discontent broke over Lincoln's head. The Republicans in the Senate, growing restive over the inaction of Federal troops, formed their own investigating committee to discover what was wrong. The powerful abolitionist senator Ben Wade of Ohio stomped to the White House to ask some characteristically blunt questions. Did McClellan favor slavery and the South? Lincoln somehow kept the peace.

McClellan's failure to move against the Confederate forces shook Lincoln's confidence in him. The President borrowed books on military science from the Library of Congress, and began to school himself in the art of war. When he wished to discuss military theory with McClellan,. the little general brushed him aside. But Lincoln picked up information that would prove invaluable to the Union cause later in the war.

Still other problems beset the President, who in his inaugural had said: "I have no purpose, directly or indirectly, to interfere with the institution of slavery in the States where it exists." In the summer of 1861 trouble came from John C. Frémont, who had been the Republican candidate for President in 1856, and was now commanding general of the Union's western forces in St. Louis. Frémont had issued a military proclamation freeing the slaves of all persons in Missouri supporting the Confederacy. Lincoln stood by his word, nullifying Frémont's proclamation and bringing down on his head the abuse of the abolitionists. When Frémont tried to

Extreme abolitionists were a constant thorn in Lincoln's side. One of their tracts carried the picture below showing, besides slavery, many other ills the South was heir to.

NEW-YORK HISTORICAL SOC

contest the President's authority, Lincoln removed him from command.

Suddenly, a war with England was threatened. The dispute grew out of the unauthorized act of a Union naval officer who boarded the *Trent*, a British mail packet, and seized two Confederate agents bound for Europe. Lincoln, while not panicking before the hostile tone of the British press, gave Secretary of State Seward sound advice: "One war at a time." The Confederate agents were released.

On top of these crises, McClellan fell ill in January of 1862, and the Federal army was paralyzed while the general languished in bed. A distracted Lincoln moaned to his Quartermaster General, "The bottom is out of the tub" and spoke "of taking the field himself."

Presently a sulky McClellan was aroused from his bed to attend a Cabinet meeting, where he remained silent. When the Quartermaster General urged the general to reveal his intentions to the President, McClellan replied most bitterly: "If I tell him my plans they will be in the *New York Herald* tomorrow morning. He can't keep a secret, he will tell them to Tad." Eventually McClellan was persuaded to admit that he had authorized a slight advance in Kentucky.

Lincoln's vexations were multiplied when he appointed Edwin McMasters Stanton to replace the incompetent Cameron as Secretary of War. Stanton, an intense, irascible man with a highly explosive personality, continually quarreled with the President. But despite this conflict, the two men had admiration and respect for each other.

A bitter personal tragedy struck next. The Lincolns were holding an official ball on the evening when young Willie came down with a mysterious illness—probably typhoid fever. Bright, humorous, and warmhearted, Willie was the son most like his father, and the two were very close. As the days dragged on with Willie now worse, now better, and worse again, Lincoln spent as much time with his son as he could.

On February 20, 1862, Willie died. Coming from his room, Lincoln spoke to his secretary in a choked voice: "Well, Nicolay, my boy is gone—he is actually gone!" The President burst into tears and walked away.

Mary Lincoln, hysterical in grief, took to her room and was seldom seen for several weeks. Her mourning was so intense and so prolonged that Lincoln feared for her sanity. She was never quite the same after the loss of Willie.

The gay, affectionate Tad was inconsolable after his brother's death. He missed Willie desperately, and sensing his father's unhappiness too, Tad turned to him for love and companionship. Lincoln and "Taddie" became inseparable—the boy played in the President's office, disrupted Cabinet meetings, and went with Lincoln whenever he journeyed into the field to review the troops.

But the President's private grief did

not obscure his wartime responsibilities. He approved the model of an ironclad ship designed by John Ericsson and authorized him to build the *Monitor* with all due haste. Information had come in that the Confederates were building an ironclad on the hull of the frigate *Merrimac* which they had salvaged after the capture of the Norfolk Navy Yard.

On March 9 an emergency meeting of the Cabinet was called. Lincoln had received disastrous news. The previous morning the ironclad *Merrimac* had steamed into Hampton Roads where a large Federal fleet of conventional wooden ships lay at anchor. She had attacked and sunk the sloop *Cumberland* and the frigate *Congress*. Some damage to the *Merrimac's* smokestack and approaching night were all that had saved the rest of the fleet.

Stanton strode around the meeting room in a wild mood, saying that it was "not unlikely [that] we shall have a shell or cannon-ball from one of her guns in the White House before we leave this room." Gloom pervaded Washington as the telegraph office announced the sinking of the two ships by the Southern ironclad.

But at dawn the next day, Ericsson's *Monitor* came puffing out to meet the *Merrimac* in a contest that ended in a modest victory. Neither ironclad had been seriously damaged, but by keeping the "Rebel Monster" from attacking the remainder of the wooden ships, the *Monitor* had protected the fleet and saved the day for the Union.

MARY TODD LINCOLN
1818–1882

THOMAS (TAD) LINCOLN
1853–1871

ROBERT TODD LINCOLN
1843–1926

A FAMILY IN THE WHITE HOUSE

THE PRESIDENT AND WILLIE

Willie Lincoln loved books and often wrote poetry with his father. After his death at 12 in 1862, gaiety left the White House. Mrs. Lincoln never stopped mourning; but the mischievous Tad, a play-actor in uniform, was often able to cheer up the President. Robert, a stylish Harvard man, could only join the family on holidays.

As April began, General McClellan was finally compelled to act. He sailed from Alexandria, Virginia, for Fort Monroe situated at the entrance to Hampton Roads at the tip of the Virginia Peninsula. The general planned to storm Richmond by marching his men up the narrow Peninsula.

However, Lincoln had given emphatic instructions that the approaches to Washington were at all times to be securely protected. The capital was the symbol of the preservation of the Union, just as Richmond symbolized the Confederacy. Therefore when Confederate General "Stonewall" Jackson threatened the Northern capital by waging a brilliant campaign in the Shenandoah Valley, the President ordered General McDowell's corps not to advance to the Peninsula where McClellan expected them. This incident, among others, outraged McClellan. He made sneering comments about "those treacherous hounds" who exercised authority in that "sink of iniquity, Washington."

Lincoln kept his temper. McClellan's forces outnumbered the Confederate troops yet he appeared to be wasting time in elaborate preparations to take thinly manned defenses. Early the following month, however, there were signs of progress. On May 4 Yorktown fell to McClellan, virtually by default. Northern gunboats steamed up the York River to West Point, Virginia, thirty-seven miles from Richmond. Next day the two armies fought in the rain at Williamsburg and the Confederates retreated, leaving their wounded on the field.

On May 6, accompanied by Stanton and Chase, Lincoln reached Fort Monroe to judge the situation for himself. He ordered an immediate attack on Norfolk and the Confederate batteries at Sewall's Point. This successful strategy opened the James River to Union gunboats which moved up to the Southern fortifications at Drewry's Bluff—only eight miles from Richmond. Chase could not disguise his elation in a letter to his daughter: "So has ended a brilliant week's campaign for the President . . . . if we had not come down, Norfolk would still have been in possession of the enemy, and the *Merrimac* as grim and defiant and as much of a terror as ever. The whole coast is now virtually ours."

Back in Washington, Lincoln waited for news of an expected Northern triumph. Meanwhile another Union general, David Hunter, took the conduct of the war into his own hands and proclaimed freedom for all the slaves in Georgia, South Carolina, and Florida. Hunter's proclamation was a practical move to swell the Union ranks with former slaves. Although Lincoln sympathized with the measure, he was still committed to his campaign promises, and wrote "No commanding general shall do such a thing, upon *my* responsibility, without consulting me." Hunter's proclamation was revoked. At the same time, however, the President made an unsuccessful appeal to the congressmen

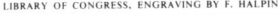

The Civil War was a test for the inventiveness and endurance of both sides. New devices were used such as observation balloons (left) and ironclads (below). But to win victories, generals were needed—leaders as brilliant as Stonewall Jackson, shown hatless above with the South's General Robert E. Lee.

Lincoln's study, the only White House room not redecorated by his wife, is seen in the picture above. Here Lincoln read war bulletins, pondered emancipation, and wrote such documents as the 1863 Thanksgiving Proclamation.

from the border states to persuade their state legislatures to free their slaves in return for fair payment from Congress for this "property."

Lincoln haunted the telegraph office in the War Department, hoping for news from McClellan. The last day of May produced the kind of dispatch the President did not want. It told of a battle at Fair Oaks (or Seven Pines) in which Confederate troops under General Joseph E. Johnston had severely damaged McClellan's forces. Johnston, however, had been wounded in the fray, and command of the reawakened Rebel forces in Virginia passed to General Robert E. Lee.

McClellan, for his part, seemed encouraged by the change in the Southern command. He informed Lincoln that he considered Lee "cautious & weak under grave responsibility."

Before another month ended McClellan would come to regret these words. From June 26 to July 2 an aggressive Lee unleashed a series of engagements known as the Seven Days' Battles. These encounters swept McClellan's army from the approaches to Richmond, and left the retreating, bewildered Federals glad to fall back to the protection of their gunboats at Harrison's Landing down the James River. McClellan, as usual, mistakenly believed that Lee's men outnumbered his own. He made yet another appeal for reinforcements on the third day of bitter fighting, and held himself blameless for the Union disaster that followed.

Lincoln, tired of telegrams, went to Harrison's Landing to judge for himself what to do next. The Union position deeply worried him. There was the possibility that the humid summer climate would debilitate the soldiers with malaria. There was McClellan's habit of overestimating the strength of the enemy. And lastly, there was McClellan's shrill insistence that he could still take Richmond if properly reinforced by the soldiers who were guarding Washington.

In early March McClellan had been relieved of his duties as general in chief, but retained command of the Army of the Potomac. On July 11, the President chose a new military advisor. General Henry W. Halleck, a military scholar and tactician, was appointed general in chief. Accompanying Lincoln to Harrison's Landing, General Halleck shared the President's apprehensions that the situation was far from reassuring.

But who besides Little Mac was capable of fighting the war that at times seemed to be totally Lincoln's concern? During the early months of 1862 many battles had been fought on the edges of the Confederacy. But which Union commander showed the most ability to fight and win? Generals—some good, some bad—were being made and broken in an unending succession. A stumpy little man from Galena, Illinois, named Ulysses S. Grant was being called a drunkard and an incompetent in the press. This was despite his spirited actions at Belmont, Missouri, and at Paducah where he stopped a Confederate advance into Kentucky. At forts Henry and Donelson, Grant had thwarted Confederate penetration into northern Tennessee. At Shiloh (Pittsburg Landing) he had forced the Rebels out of Tennessee and back into Mississippi. But Halleck, Grant's superior officer, had taken credit for most of Grant's victories.

Even more obscure was William Tecumseh Sherman. He had the trying job of holding the state of Kentucky with nothing but raw recruits. Always a nervous person, he tended (like McClellan) to overestimate the strength and position of the Confederates. But Sherman later proved himself to be a superior military leader.

Another general who won perhaps undeserved recognition was John

AMERICAN ANTIQUARIAN SOCIETY

THE ENEMY IS APPROACHING!

I MUST RELY UPON THE PEOPLE FOR THE

DEFENCE of the STATE!

AND HAVE Called THE MILITIA for that PURPOSE!

A. G. CURTIN, Governor of Pennsylvania.

THE TERM OF SERVICE WILL ONLY BE WHILE THE DANGER OF THE STATE IS IMMINENT.

APPLY AT

FALSTAFF HOTEL, N.W. cor. 6th & Jayne

Capt. JOHN McCORMACK.

J. CARTER, 1st Lieut.

Two notable Union victories occurred in 1862 and 1863 when Confederate invaders (above) were repulsed in the North. The first was the Battle of Antietam; McClellan's forces charged, pummeled the Southern line (right), but did not follow through. The second victory was Gettysburg.

Pope. Marching on Tennessee in April of 1862, Pope and 17,000 men reached the Missouri shore of the Mississippi River, but were prevented from crossing by a Confederate battery commanding the Tennessee side. Pope asked for help from Andrew H. Foote who commanded the Union's ironclad river fleet.

But the heavily fortified Confederate stronghold of Island No. 10 in the middle of the river held Foote back. Finally the ironclad gunboat *Carondelet* managed to sneak past the island in a wild thunderstorm to meet Pope's forces. Joined by another gunboat the next day, the ironclads destroyed the Rebel battery, and Pope's men crossed the river. Island No. 10 was then cut off from supplies and surrendered soon after. This permitted the Union ironclads to move downriver to Memphis, destroy a Confederate fleet and take the city.

Pope was acclaimed for this victory, and put in charge of the newly created Army of Virginia. McClellan was ordered to abandon the Peninsula Campaign and return to Washington to reinforce Pope's men against Lee.

In the meantime Lincoln had been wrestling with an issue even more important than generals—the question of slavery. In early June the President began visiting the War Department, where he used the desk of Thomas T. Eckert, general superintendent of the military telegraph. In fascination Eckert watched Lincoln at work: "He would look out of the window a while and then put his pen to paper, but he did not write much at once. He would study between times and when he had made up his mind he would put down a line or two, and then sit quiet for a few minutes...."

For several weeks the President repeated this performance. Then, at the end of July, he told his Cabinet the purpose behind these labors. If the South persisted in the war, the President said, then he planned to free the slaves. A little earlier he had told Secretary of the Navy Welles that "he had given it much thought and had about come to the conclusion that it

119

was a military necessity absolutely essential for the salvation of the Union, that we must free the slaves or be ourselves subdued."

The Cabinet received the proposition soberly. Seward told the President that he heartily approved of its sentiment. But he went on to say that such a proclamation should not be issued without a military success to support it or else the public would consider the proclamation "the last measure of an exhausted government."

Lincoln agreed. He locked up the draft of his proclamation, awaiting the appropriate moment. In August Lee, supported by Stonewall Jackson, closed in for a second battle at Manassas Junction, Virginia. General Pope's military talent proved insufficient to match Lee's tactical genius.

John Hay described the President as he waited for a favorable report during the long hours of battle: "Everything seemed to be going well and hilarious on Saturday and we went to bed expecting glad tidings at sunrise. But about eight o'clock the President came to my room as I was dressing and, calling me out, said, 'Well, John, we are whipped again, I am afraid. The enemy reinforced on Pope and drove back his left wing and he has retired to Centreville where he says he will be able to hold his men. I don't like that expression. I don't like to hear him admit that his men need *holding*.'"

Lincoln had good reason for his fears, for Pope's army of 90,000 men had been roundly beaten by Lee's 55,000 Confederates. Fear swept again through Washington as the Federals fell back into the capital's entrenchments. But Lee, himself exhausted, did not follow up this success with a spirited pursuit. Instead, Lee carried the war into the North by invading Maryland in early September. Lincoln, sick of Pope, and having really no other choice, restored McClellan's army to him.

A copy of Lee's orders was found by one of McClellan's men, giving the Federals a chance to attack Lee's scattered forces. But McClellan moved too slowly. Lee was allowed time to concentrate his army at Antietam Creek in Maryland, and on September 17 a bloody, indecisive battle was fought. Although McClellan did not attack on the eighteenth, that night the Confederates, weary and dangerously weakened by their losses, fell back into Virginia—ending the invasion.

But even this half victory gave Lincoln the opportunity for which he had been waiting. On Monday, September 22, five days after the battle at Antietam Creek, he issued the first, or preliminary, Proclamation of Emancipation. It warned that if states, or parts of states, then in rebellion did not return to the Union by January 1, 1863, he would issue a second proclamation declaring the slaves in such regions to be "forever free."

The Emancipation Proclamation (right) was Lincoln's first step against slavery—it freed all slaves of masters rebelling against the Union. Passage of the Thirteenth Amendment in 1865 ended slavery in America.

EMANCIPATION PROCLAMATION

ISSUED JANUARY 1ST 1863.

8 THE WAY TO VICTORY

For a month after the Battle of Antietam, McClellan sent excuses to Lincoln for his continued failure to pursue Lee into Richmond. The President's patience finally wore out, and the modest, bewhiskered General Ambrose E. Burnside was ordered to take over McClellan's command. But Burnside doubted seriously that he had the talent to lead the entire army—and he was right.

Lee's 78,000 men entrenched themselves on Marye's Heights behind the city of Fredericksburg, Virginia. Burnside ordered a suicidal frontal assault and lost 9,000 of his 122,000 men. Lincoln was agonized when he learned the cost of Burnside's tragic blunder. The North reeled under this terrible blow, and army desertions increased. Newspapers demanded the resignations of various Cabinet members, and some Republican senators believed Lincoln should resign.

As January 1, 1863, drew near, the public asked another question: would Lincoln really sign the Emancipation Proclamation? That muddy, dismal New Year's Day, Lincoln shook hands for three hours with callers at the White House. When he reached his office in midafternoon his right hand was limp and swollen.

Only a few dignitaries were on hand to witness the signing. Never,

The 1864 cartoon at left shows McClellan, by then out of command, counseling Lincoln against letting Grant (the "old bulldog") advance down the railway to Richmond.

123

HENRY W. HALLECK    AMBROSE E. BURNSIDE    JOSEPH HOOKER    GEORGE G. MEADE

After McClellan failed him, Lincoln appointed the brilliant Henry W. Halleck as his chief military advisor. To press the fight in the East, Lincoln tried in turn Ambrose Burnside, "Fighting Joe" Hooker, and the respected George Meade.

Lincoln said, had he been more certain of doing right and he hoped a trembling signature would not be interpreted as showing hesitancy. "But anyway it is going to be done!" he declared. Slowly he signed his full name.

Lincoln's search for a general who could defeat Lee continued. In Joseph Hooker he knew that he was picking a drinker and a braggart, but Hooker could fight. "Beware of rashness," the President warned, "but with energy, and sleepless vigilance, go forward and give us victories."

In April, visiting Hooker's headquarters, Lincoln looked through field glasses at the battle-scarred city of Fredericksburg. He and Tad reviewed the troops whose morale had been lifted by Hooker's confidence in them. The general assured Lincoln that his 130,000 troops thrown against Lee's 60,000 would win a quick, decisive victory.

But early May brought disaster to the Union army at Chancellorsville. The President, an old hand by now at reading war telegrams, realized at once that the Federal attack had been badly coordinated. How thoroughly beaten Hooker had been could not be disguised from Lincoln. Head bent, hands clasped behind his back, he paced the floor of his office moaning: "My God! My God! What will the country say? What *will* the country say?"

Yet bad news never defeated Lincoln for long. An amusing story would revive his spirits, and an adventure with Tad would completely restore his hope and strength. Donning his tall hat, he would reach for Tad's hand and set off into everyday Washington.

Sometimes they would visit the lady

who sold gingerbread and apples on Pennsylvania Avenue. Or, a little way down the street, they would stop for a while with the telescope man whose sign offered "Five cents to look at the stars, ten cents to look at the moon." Or, best of all, they would drop in on the toymaker Joseph Stuntz, an old campaigner who had fought in Napoleon's army. His beautifully carved toys, and especially his wooden soldiers, delighted Tad and his father.

Although Tad gave Lincoln joyful companionship, the President's relations with his eldest son were strained. Robert, then an earnest young man of twenty, begged his father for permission to leave Harvard and join the army. It was refused. Seeing how deeply Willie's death had disturbed his wife, Lincoln feared that another loss might kill her. Finally, in early 1865, Lincoln found a staff position for his son, and Captain Robert Lincoln began a useful career in the army.

The spring of 1863 finally brought victorious news to the anxious President. Reducing war to four words—"When in doubt, fight!"—General Grant had conducted a brilliant campaign against Vicksburg, the Confederacy's guardian of the lower Mississippi.

Grant had shifted his troops down the western side of the river to a rendezvous with transports which had run past the blazing batteries on Vicksburg's high bluffs. Then striking inland, he had separated two Rebel armies and bottled up 30,000 Confed-

The best news of 1863 was the success of U. S. Grant in the West. In this Brady photograph, Grant looks rumpled but determined.

THIS HALLOWED GROUND

Lincoln had little time to prepare his speech for the dedication of the Gettysburg cemetery. On the morning of November 19, 1863, he recopied his address (right), and rode out to the cemetery with a crowd of 15,000 (below). Circled in white in the bottom photograph, Lincoln is about to begin speaking.

ABOVE: NATIONAL PARK SERVICE—BELOW: NATIONAL ARCHIVES

erate soldiers within Vicksburg. On May 22, his second attempt to storm Vicksburg failed, and Grant ordered his troops to entrench and besiege the city until it surrendered.

In mid-May Lee had been called to a Cabinet meeting in Richmond. Could he detach part of his army to save Vicksburg? With his men barefoot, and without food or fodder for their horses, Lee was forced to say no. But a new and daring plan was drawn up. Lee would strike north into the bountiful farmlands of Pennsylvania. Doing this he could reprovision his army, and relieve pressure on Vicksburg as Union troops were shifted to meet him.

Lee started north on June 3 and panic raced through Pennsylvania, Maryland, and New Jersey. General Hooker demanded immediate reinforcements to meet the Confederate invasion. But General in Chief Halleck refused, finding it strategically important that troops in the northeast remain where they were. In the crisis Hooker resigned, and President Lincoln replaced him with General George Gordon Meade. A stern, quick-tempered man, Meade possessed the advantage of fighting in defense of his own home soil. Lee, uninformed of the whereabouts of the Union army, met Meade's forces unexpectedly at the little town of Gettysburg, Pennsylvania, on July 1.

For three terrible days the battle raged. Although the Confederates won the first skirmish, the Union troops managed to dig in on Cemetery

Ridge and on July 3 cut down a wild, daring charge of 15,000 Confederates led by Major General George Pickett. At this point Lee had lost more than 20,000 men—nearly a third of his army—in a vicious battle that was to turn the tide of the war against him. Staggered, Lee retreated toward Virginia, wondering how he would fight his way across the Potomac.

Lincoln also wondered how Lee's army could escape. General Meade pursued Lee, but with his own losses running to 23,000 men he was unwilling to attack the Confederates.

The President poured out his heart to his Secretary of the Navy. "There is bad faith somewhere. Meade has been pressed and urged, but only one of his generals was for immediate attack, was ready to pounce on Lee; the rest held back. What does it mean, Mr. Welles? Great God! what does it mean?"

Welles blamed Halleck who in a few hours could have journeyed from Washington to Gettysburg to judge the situation for himself. In character, Lincoln defended his general in chief: "It is better that I, who am not a military man, should defer to him, rather than he to me." Yet Lincoln had seen that Meade, too, had failed him.

On July 7, four days after the Union victory at Gettysburg, Lincoln learned that Vicksburg had surrendered to Grant. At last the able soldier received the national acclaim he had so long deserved. And the President, though he did not yet realize it, was very close to finding the man of success that the Union so desperately needed.

The movement to erect a cemetery at Gettysburg began immediately after the battle. On November 19 the cemetery was ready for a dedication ceremony. Edward Everett of Massachusetts, then acknowledged as America's finest orator, was to be the main speaker. Almost at the last moment Lincoln was asked to say a few words.

When the President's turn to speak came, he stood, looked down on the neat rows of graves of those who had fallen in the battle, and in a clear, firm voice, began:

"Fourscore and seven years ago our fathers brought forth on this continent, a new nation, conceived in liberty, and dedicated to the proposition that all men are created equal. Now we are engaged in a great civil war, testing whether that nation, or any nation so conceived and so dedicated, can long endure. . . ."

Yet despite Lincoln's eloquent leadership and the Gettysburg and Vicksburg victories, the costly war went on. There was widespread discontent over the Union Conscription Act of 1863 which made all males between eighteen and forty-five subject to military service for three years. However, the Act exempted a man if he could afford to hire a replacement or pay $300. In July resentment over this exemption clause among New York City's thousands of impoverished laborers

The North was weary of continual military setbacks in the election year of 1864, and Lincoln doubted that he would be re-elected. The Republicans named Andrew Johnson to run with him and adopted a platform stressing union and quick victory as seen in the campaign poster above.

THE TRUE ISSUE OR "THATS WHATS THE MATTER".

As Lincoln and Jeff Davis seek to tear the Union apart in this cartoon, McClellan, the Democratic candidate in 1864, indicates that the issues are not worth any more bloodshed.

touched off six violent days of bloodshed, lynching of Negroes, and burning and looting of property.

In August, bandit raiders under William Clarke Quantrill, ex-schoolteacher, horse thief, and Confederate sympathizer, brought death and destruction to Lawrence, Kansas. A federal fleet that had been besieging Charleston, South Carolina, since April was still stalled. Then in September, after managing to capture Chattanooga, Tennessee, a Federal army under the leadership of General William Starke Rosecrans was smashed apart during the Battle of Chickamauga.

To avoid complete disaster in Tennessee, Lincoln turned to the man who had captured Vicksburg—Major General Ulysses S. Grant. Despite a bad leg injured in a fall from a horse, the energetic Grant reorganized the dispirited troops and then opened up the Confederate stranglehold on the Union supply lines. On the twenty-fifth of November, after inspired fighting along Missionary Ridge outside of Chattanooga, Tennessee, General Grant's men shattered the Confederate army and hurled it back into Georgia.

Lincoln knew he had found his general at last. By special congressional action the rank of lieutenant general, previously held only by George Washington and Winfield Scott, was revived for Grant. In March of 1864 he arrived in Washington to take command of Federal armies numbering more than a half million men. He met Lincoln at the White House as guests climbed onto chairs and sofas to catch a glimpse of the short, rugged hero.

Lincoln understood and trusted Grant from the first—they were both go-ahead Westerners. When Grant suggested bringing General Philip H. Sheridan east to command his cavalry, Lincoln wondered aloud if Sheridan was not "rather a little fellow." Grant replied firmly: "You will find him big enough for the purpose."

Grant moved quickly to formulate a plan to end the war. In May while Federal forces under General William Tecumseh Sherman swept down from Tennessee to capture Atlanta, Georgia, Grant tangled with Lee in Virginia. General Lee had put his troops behind breastworks in a dense, marshy forest known as the Wilderness. And though his men were badly outnumbered, they had the advantage of his military genius and knowledge of the terrain.

But Grant, despite an incredible loss of life that gained him the nickname of "the butcher," hammered continually at Lee's defenses for over a month. He wired the President saying, "I propose to fight it out on this line if it takes all summer." Lee realized that Grant's reputation of never giving up was well earned and sensed that, unless a miracle intervened, the tenacious little man would hang on until he won.

In an attempt to get around Lee's flank, Grant kept moving his troops southward. With staggering losses Grant fought Lee at Spotsylvania, Cold Harbor, and Petersburg. Going after Lee's supply and communication routes, Grant dug in for a siege at Petersburg. Keeping after Lee constantly, Grant never relaxed pressure on the Confederate lines.

Early in July, attempting to shake off Grant's bulldog bite, Lee sent Confederate forces under General Jubal Early to attack Washington once again. By July 12 Early had been driven from the outskirts of Washington. He was pursued through the Shenandoah Valley and eventually defeated by Major General Phil Sheridan. To prevent the Confederates from using the valley again as a route north, Grant ordered Sheridan to destroy it completely. His order was carried out with grim efficiency. In the meantime the wily maneuverings of Confederate General Joe Johnston had General William Tecumseh Sherman fighting in delaying actions instead of marching directly on Atlanta.

Discouraging war news and heavy casualties did not help the Republican party in the election year of 1864. Hoping to quiet radical Northern agitation against Lincoln and to at-

Grant and Lincoln first met at a White House reception. In the painting above, the Presiden reets Mrs. Grant as the general looks on. Mrs. Lincoln (far right) sits with General Scott.

tract "War Democrats," the Republicans labeled themselves the Union Party. Despite protests against Lincoln's handling of the war, he was renominated. Tennessee's Democratic, pro-war governor, Andrew Johnson was named as his running mate.

But the Republicans remained divided over the candidacy of Lincoln. The week before the national convention, a small splinter party of Republican radical die-hards gathered in Cleveland to nominate John C. Frémont for President. And in August the Democrats—their antiwar "Copperhead" wing powerful and vocal—met in Chicago to make General George B. McClellan their standard-bearer.

Lincoln versus his disenchanted generals—how did the President feel? Although Frémont's candidacy rallied radical antislavery men against him, McClellan was Lincoln's greatest worry. With Grant stalemated before Lee at Petersburg, and Sherman seemingly bogged down in his drive on Atlanta, Lincoln believed that he could not be re-elected.

Just as the situation seemed the darkest to Lincoln, he received word that Admiral David G. Farragut had led the Union navy to a sweeping victory in Mobile Bay on August 5. Then, on September 1, came the news that Atlanta had surrendered to General Sherman.

In late September, after bargaining for the removal of ultra-conservative Montgomery Blair from the Cabinet, Frémont withdrew from the race. In October, state elections in Ohio, Indiana, and Pennsylvania backed the Republicans and gave a strong indication of how the national election would go.

On the gloomy, wet evening of November 8, Lincoln waited anxiously in the telegraph office for the first returns. Toward midnight the trend was clear—except for Kentucky, Delaware, and New Jersey, Lincoln had carried the election. As the victory became clear, John Hay said, "the President went awkwardly and hospitably to work shovelling out the fried oysters."

In December the Lincolns enjoyed their first happy Christmas in a long while: The President had won re-election, and the war news was encouraging. General Sherman's army was cutting a sixty-mile swath of destruction through the heart of Georgia from Atlanta to Savannah, and the collapse of the Confederacy was near. As he was hoping that the new year would bring an end to the war, Lincoln was handed a telegram from Sherman reading, "I beg to present you as a Christmas gift the city of Savannah."

But the President realized that a new and deeper understanding of the word freedom as well as successful military campaigns was necessary if the war were to be truly won. Lincoln refused to be discouraged by the fact that the previous year the House had failed to pass the Thirteenth Amendment abolishing slavery. Now he intended to force a reconsideration of the amendment, and his maneuvering behind the scenes was masterful.

Charles Dana, the Assistant Secretary of War, described him: "Lincoln was a supreme politician. He understood politics because he understood human nature.... There was no flabby philanthropy about Abraham Lincoln. He was all solid, hard, keen intelligence combined with goodness. ... The expression of his face and of his bearing which impressed one most, after his benevolence and benignity, was his intelligent understanding. You felt that here was a man who saw through things, who understood, and you respected him accordingly."

Realizing that passage of the amendment would mean at least a million more men in the field, Lincoln told Representative James S. Rollins of Missouri, "The passage of this amendment will clinch the whole subject. It will bring the war, I have no doubt, rapidly to a close."

When the measure came to a vote on the last day of January, 1865, Cabinet members, justices of the Supreme Court, and senators jammed the galleries and crowded the entrance to the House of Representatives. As the roll call ended, the tally showed that the amendment had passed by three votes. For ten minutes people danced, cheered, and embraced.

The next night a torchlight parade gathered at the White House to serenade the President. He came out on a

This Union view of the Great Emancipator appeared in 1862; but the shackles of all American slaves did not open until the Thirteenth Amendment was passed by Congress.

balcony to speak and a member of the crowd recalled him saying that "He wished the reunion of all the States perfected, and so effected as to remove all causes of disturbances in the future; and, to attain this end, it was necessary that the original disturbing cause should, if possible, be rooted out.... But this amendment is a king's cure-all for all evils. It winds the whole thing up.... He could not but congratulate all present—himself, the country, and the whole world—upon this great moral victory."

9 WITH MALICE TOWARD

On March 4, 1865, Lincoln went to his second inauguration. Men with one arm, one leg watched him—veterans of the struggle to save the Union. The ghastly cost of the war was constantly on the President's mind, haunting his sleep, his conscience.

As Lincoln came forward to speak, the sun broke through a day heavy with rain. He spoke movingly of the war and of slavery: "Neither party expected for the war the magnitude or the duration which it has already attained.... Each looked for an easier triumph, and a result less fundamental and astounding.... Fondly do we hope—fervently do we pray—that this mightly scourge of war may speedily pass away. Yet if God wills that it continue until... every drop of blood drawn with the lash shall be paid by another drawn with the sword... 'The judgments of the Lord are true and righteous altogether.'"

Lincoln ended his brief address with the words: "With malice toward none;

Just before the last campaign of the war, Lincoln conferred with his military leaders at City Point, Virginia. Shown from left to right in G. P. A. Healy's painting are Sherman, Grant, Lincoln, and Admiral Porter.

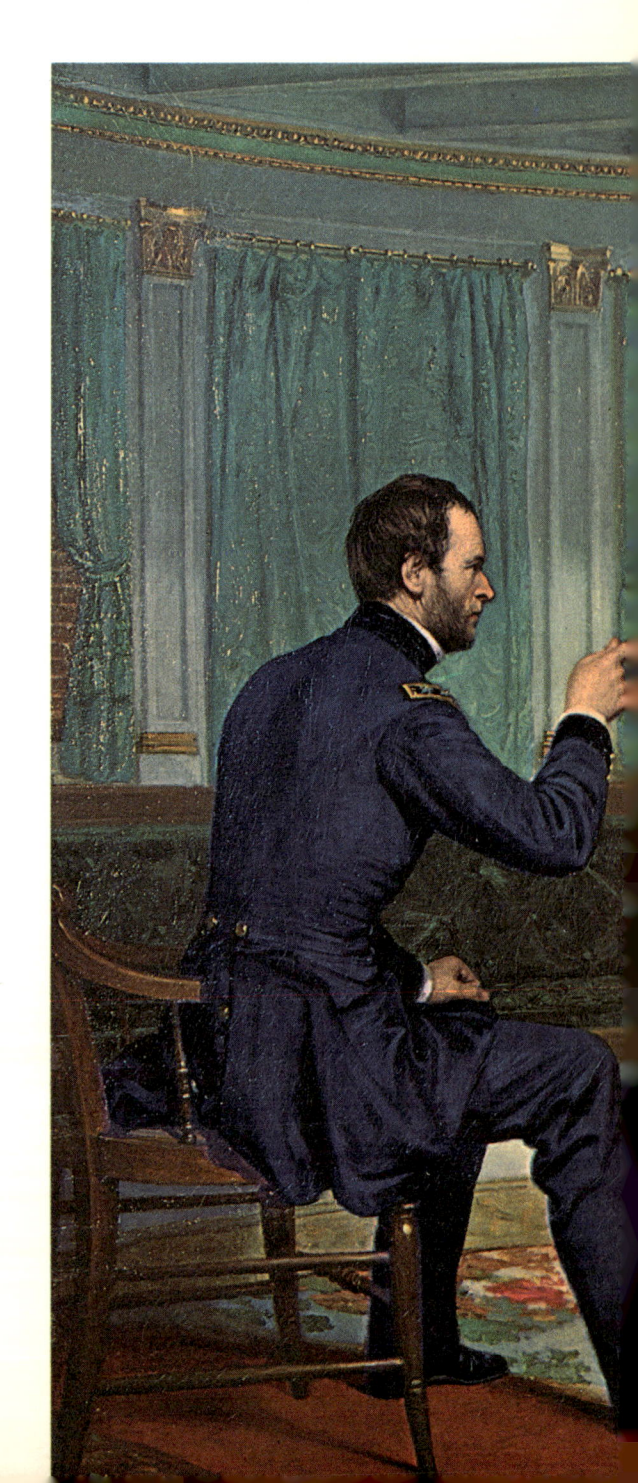

NONE

WHITE HOUSE COLLECTION, COURTESY WHITE HOUSE HISTORICAL ASSOCIATION

with charity for all; with firmness in the right, as God gives us to see the right, let us strive on to finish the work we are in; to bind up the nation's wounds; to care for him who shall have borne the battle, and for his widow, and his orphan—to do all which may achieve and cherish a just and lasting peace among ourselves, and with all nations."

On March 20, 1865, the President, Mrs. Lincoln, and Tad went to City Point, Virginia, for a visit to General Grant's headquarters. Lincoln, "his face haggard with care and seamed with thought and trouble," as Horace Greeley described him, was glad to go. He needed a respite from his Washington duties, and hoped that a conference with his military leaders might speedily conclude the war.

For the first time the three Western men were together—the tired, thin Lincoln, the lean, intent Sherman, and the calm, determined Grant. Was there a chance of ending the war without another battle, the President asked. Grant thought not. Yet, leaving City Point, Grant told an aide: "I think we can send him some good news in a day or two."

The end came quickly. Sherman continued his successful campaign against General Joe Johnston's forces in North Carolina. And Grant took Petersburg, Lee's last line of defense, on April 2. The victorious Grant wired the good news to Lincoln at City Point and invited the President to join him. Lincoln arrived the following day and was met by his son Robert with a mounted escort. The next morning Lincoln entered Richmond, left burning and abandoned by Confederate leaders.

Negroes surrounded the President, thanking and welcoming him. Admiral David Porter heard Lincoln tell them: "Don't kneel to me. That is not right. You must kneel to God only, and thank Him for the liberty you will hereafter enjoy. I am but God's humble instrument; but you may rest assured that as long as I live no one shall put a shackle to your limbs, and you shall have all the rights which God has given to every other free citizen of this Republic."

Back in the White House on the evening of April 9, Lincoln received news of Lee's surrender to Grant at Appomattox Court House, Virginia. The next morning Washington was wild with joy and the President promised to speak the following day. He addressed the huge crowd gathered on the White House lawn soberly.

Lincoln spoke of the problems of reconstruction which he knew to be "fraught with great difficulty." He made a plea for forgiveness, and asked, "Let us all join in doing the acts necessary to restoring the proper practical relations between these states and the Union."

On Friday morning, April 14, 1865, Lincoln attended his last Cabinet meeting. The matter at hand was reconstruction. "There are men in Congress," remarked the President, "who

Harper's Weekly, JANUARY 3, 1863

COLUMBIA. "Where are my 15,000 Sons—murdered at Fredericksburg?" LINCOLN. "This reminds me of a little Joke—" COLUMBIA. "Go tell your Joke AT SPRINGFIELD!!"

SURRENDER OF GEN. LEE!

"The Year of Jubilee has come! Let all the People Rejoice!"

200 GUNS WILL BE FIRED

On the Campus Martius,
AT 3 O'CLOCK TO-DAY, APRIL 10,
To Celebrate the Victories of our Armies.

Every Man, Woman and Child is hereby ordered to be on hand prepared to Sing and Rejoice. The crowd are expected to join in singing Patriotic Songs.
ALL PLACES OF BUSINESS MUST BE CLOSED AT 2 O'CLOCK.
Hurrah for Grant and his noble Army.

By Order of the People.

DETROIT PUBLIC LIBRARY

In this 1863 cartoon, Columbia, symbol of America, accuses Lincoln, a general, and Secretary of War Stanton of having squandered her sons in the three-year assault on Richmond. But two years later, when the joyous poster at left appeared in Detroit, the nation was cheering the President and Grant.

OVERLEAF: *Although this painting shows the carriage ride Lincoln and Admiral Porter took through the streets of Richmond as a jubilant tour, few citizens of the fallen capital rejoiced in the Northern victory. As one Richmond woman said, "We covered our faces and cried aloud."*

CHICAGO HISTORICAL SOCIETY

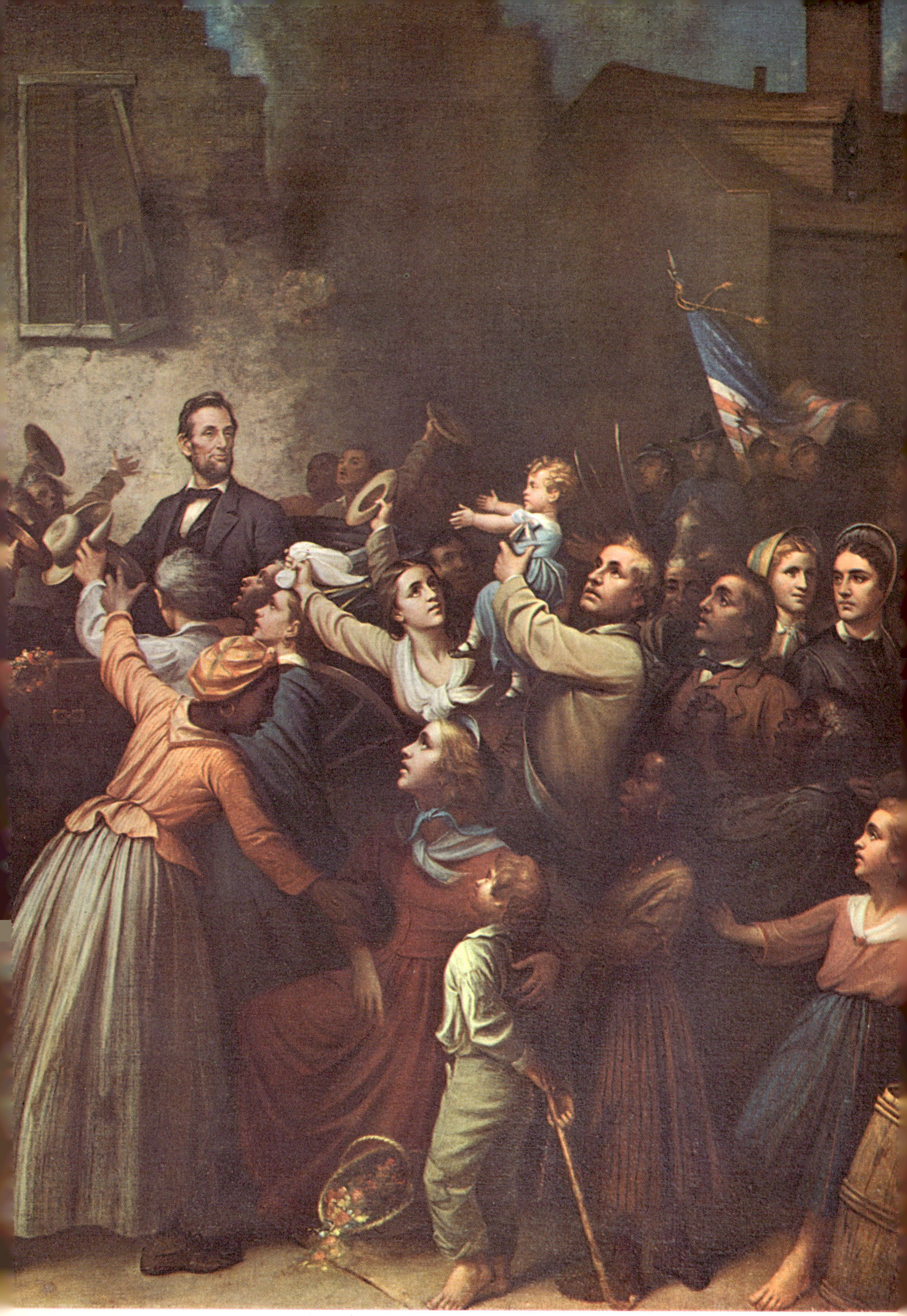

A humorous and kindly man, Lincoln once said of himself: "If I couldn't tell [comical] stories I would die." This photograph was taken shortly before the rugged Illinoisan had won the presidential election of 1860.

possess feelings of hate and vindictiveness in which I do not sympathize and cannot participate." When discussion turned to the reorganization of the governments of the defeated Southern states Lincoln said, "We can't undertake to run State governments in all these Southern States. Their people must do that—though I reckon that at first some may do it badly."

The Cabinet inquired anxiously whether the President had heard any news from General Sherman. Lincoln and Grant hourly expected news of Johnston's surrender, and the President had already paid one visit to the War Department that morning. Secretary Welles wrote in his diary that "The President remarked it would, he had no doubt, come soon, and come favorable, for he had last night the usual dream which he had preceding nearly every great and important event of the War."

This was not the only dream that had come to Lincoln in the last days of the war. Shortly after his return from Richmond he told Mrs. Lincoln a strange story. "About ten days ago," he said, "I retired very late. . . . I soon began to dream. There seemed to be a death-like stillness about me. Then I heard subdued sobs. . . . I went from room to room; no living person was in sight, but the same mournful sounds of distress met me as I passed along. . . . Determined to find the cause of a state of things so mysterious and so shocking, I kept on until I arrived at the East Room. . . . Before me was a catafalque, on which rested a corpse wrapped in funeral vestments. Around it were stationed soldiers who were acting as guards; and there was a throng of people, some gazing mournfully upon the corpse, whose face was covered, others weeping pitifully. 'Who is dead in the White House?' I demanded of one of the soldiers. 'The President,' was his answer; 'he was killed by an assassin!'" Mrs. Lincoln was quite upset by the story, and though the President attempted to reassure her, he was obviously troubled.

In the afternoon after the Cabinet meeting, Lincoln went for a drive with his wife. "Mary" he said, "we have had a hard time of it since we came to Washington, but the war is over, and with God's blessing we may hope for four years of peace and happiness, and then we will go back to Illinois and pass the rest of our lives in quiet."

That night, accompanied by two friends, the Lincolns went to Ford's Theatre to see "Our American Cousin," a play which featured the actress Laura Keene. A few minutes after ten John Wilkes Booth, an actor and Confederate sympathizer with a twisted mind, crept into the presidential box. He held a knife in one hand, a pistol in the other. He fired once. The President slumped forward. A woman screamed, and all eyes turned toward the Lincolns' box. Booth jumped to the stage, breaking a leg as he landed, and escaped through the wings.

In a coma from which he would

THE MESERVE COLLECTION

A compassionate, firm-minded President, Lincoln had suffered too much not to show exhaustion and care in his face at war's end. This last photograph of him was taken by Alexander Gardner on April 11, 1865.

143

LIBRARY OF CONG

ANNE S. K. BROWN MILITARY COLLECT

never awaken, Lincoln was gently carried across the street to the house of William Peterson and laid on a bed in a small downstairs room.

Mrs. Lincoln, weeping hysterically, had to be led into the parlor. Robert rushed to his father's side only to learn that there was no hope of recovery. Shocked and grief-stricken, he broke into tears. Ashen-faced, the Cabinet members arrived to spend the long night's vigil. When the President's labored breathing ceased at 7:22 on the morning of April 15, a profound silence filled the room. Then Secretary Stanton said softly: "Now he belongs to the ages."

The nation, divided by four bloody years of conflict, was united in the final tragedy of the war. Americans North and South mourned the death of Abraham Lincoln.

In a scene much like the one in the dream, the body of the President lay in state in the East Room of the White House. After the funeral on Wednesday, April 19, a procession of forty thousand mourners escorted Lincoln on his last journey to the Capitol.

On Friday morning, April 21, the President's coffin, along with the smaller coffin of his son Willie, was put aboard a special funeral train that was to take him home to Springfield. The slowly moving, black-draped train retraced his journey of four years before. Millions of grieving people came out to watch Lincoln's

The prints at left show the assassination of Lincoln, and the President's funeral cortege as it winds through New York. The commemorative ribbon at right was issued after his death.

funeral train as it moved slowly by.

So Abraham Lincoln came home to live forever in the hearts of the American people. His place there has always been unique—in his own time people believed that he had liberated mankind just as surely as Christ had saved it. This sentiment, which has yet to die, is remembered in the words of Julia Ward Howe's hymn, "The Battle Hymn of the Republic," the militant tune that Lincoln loved best of all the war's marching songs.

The second and fourth stanzas of that familiar hymn run as follows:

"I have seen Him in the watch fires
   of a hundred circling camps;
They have builded Him an altar in
   the evening dews and damps;
I can read His righteous sentence by
   the dim and flaring lamps,
His day is marching on.

In the beauty of the lillies Christ
   was born across the sea,
With a glory in his bosom that transfigures you and me;
As he died to make men holy, let us
   die to make men free,
While God is marching on."

Surrounding the Lincoln Memorial in Washington are 36 columns representing the states of the Union he fought so hard to re-unite. Within is the pensive statue at right.

IN THIS TEMPLE
AS IN THE HEARTS OF THE PEOPLE
FOR WHOM HE SAVED THE UNION
THE MEMORY OF ABRAHAM LINCOLN
IS ENSHRINED FOREVER

ACKNOWLEDGMENTS

The editors are indebted to the following individuals and institutions for their generous assistance in preparing this book:

Abraham Lincoln Book Shop, Chicago—Ralph G. Newman
Mrs. Anne S. K. Brown, Providence
Alexander McCook Craighead, Dayton, Ohio
Chicago Historical Society—Mrs. Mary Frances Rhymer
Chicago & Illinois Midland Railway Company, Springfield—J. E. Dare
Illinois State Historical Library, Springfield—James T. Hickey
Library of Congress, Washington—Virginia Daiker, Carl Stang
Lincoln National Life Foundation, Fort Wayne, Indiana—Ruth P. Higgins
Vincennes University, Vincennes, Indiana—Ralph F. Meeks
White House Historical Association—Nash Castro

AMERICAN HERITAGE PUBLISHING CO., INC.

PRESIDENT JAMES PARTON
EDITOR IN CHIEF JOSEPH J. THORNDIKE, JR.
EDITORIAL DIRECTOR, BOOK DIVISION RICHARD M. KETCHUM
ART DIRECTOR IRWIN GLUSKER

AMERICAN HERITAGE JUNIOR LIBRARY

MANAGING EDITOR **RUSSELL BOURNE**
ART DIRECTOR ELEANOR A. DYE
CHIEF PICTURE RESEARCHER JULIA POTTS GREHAN
PICTURE RESEARCHER MARY LEVERTY
COPY EDITOR BARBARA FISHER SHOR
EDITORIAL ASSISTANT NANCY SIMON
EDITORIAL ASSISTANT BETSY SANDERS

This wood carving of Lincoln is thought to be the work of a freed slave in Kentucky.

ABBY ALDRICH ROCKEFELLER FOLK ART COLLECTION

FOR FURTHER READING

Angle, Paul M., *Abraham Lincoln's Speeches and Letters, 1832–1865.* New York, Everyman's Library, 1957.

Angle, Paul M., *The Lincoln Reader.* New Brunswick, Rutgers University Press, 1947.

Basler, Roy P., *The Collected Works of Abraham Lincoln.* 9 vols. New Brunswick, Rutgers University Press, 1953.

Catton, Bruce, *The American Heritage Picture History of the Civil War.* New York, American Heritage Publishing Co., Inc., 1960.

Catton, Bruce, *The Battle of Gettysburg.* New York, American Heritage Publishing Co., Inc., 1963.

Donald, David, *Lincoln Reconsidered.* New York, Vintage Books, 1961.

Donovan, Frank R., *Ironclads of the Civil War.* New York, American Heritage Publishing Co., Inc., 1964.

Herndon, William H., and Weik, Jesse W., *Life of Lincoln.* New York, Living Age Books, World Publishing Co.

Lewis, Lloyd, *Myths After Lincoln.* New York, Universal Library, 1960.

Miers, Earl Schenck, *Lincoln Day by Day.* 3 vols. Washington, Lincoln Sesquicentennial Commission, 1960.

Mitgang, Herbert, *Lincoln As They Saw Him.* New York, Rinehart & Co., Inc., 1956.

Nicolay, John, and Hay, John, *Abraham Lincoln: A History.* New York, Century Co., 1914.

Randall, James G., *Lincoln the President.* 4 vols. New York, Dodd, Mead & Co., Inc., 1952.

Randall, Ruth Painter, *Lincoln's Sons.* Boston, Little, Brown & Co., 1955.

Sandburg, Carl, *Abraham Lincoln: The Prairie Years.* 2 vols. New York, Harcourt, Brace & Company, 1925–1926.

Sandburg, Carl, *Abraham Lincoln: The War Years.* 4 vols. New York, Harcourt, Brace & Company, 1936–1939.

Sherwood, Robert E., *Abe Lincoln in Illinois.* New York, Charles Scribner's Sons, 1939.

Thomas, Benjamin P., *Abraham Lincoln: A Biography.* New York, Alfred A. Knopf, 1952.

Warren, Louis A., *Lincoln's Youth: Indiana Years, 1816–1830.* New York, Appleton-Century-Crofts, Inc., 1959.

Yoseloff, Thomas, *Battles and Leaders of the Civil War.* 4 vols. New York, Thomas Yoseloff, Inc., 1956.

Pictured standing before a replica of Abraham Lincoln's first home are his two cousins, John and Dennis Hanks.

INDEX

Bold face indicates pages on which illustrations appear

Abolitionists, 38–40, 54, 64, 110
Alabama, secession of, 83
Alexandria, Va., 100, 114
Anderson, Robert, 92, **97**
Antietam, Battle of, **118**, 118–119, 120, 123
Appomattox Court House, Va., 138
Archimedes, 39
Arkansas, secession of, 100
Armies,
   Confederate, 98, **98**
   desertions in, 123
   recruitment of, 97, 99, 100, 128
   Union, 99, 100, 107, **108–109**, 114, 117, 127, 131
Armstrong, Duff, 59, 60
Armstrong, Hannah, 59, 60
Armstrong, Jack, 7, 27, 28, **32–33**, 59
Army of the Potomac, 103, **104–105**, 107, 117
Army of Virginia, 118
Arnold, Isaac N., 58
Atlanta, Ga., 131, 134
Bates, Edward, 76, 79
Beauregard, P. G. T., 92, 96, **97**
Bell, John, 78
Berry, William F., 29
Black Hawk, 29, **29**
Blair, Montgomery, 134
Bodmer, Carl, painting by, **16–17**
Booth, John Wilkes, 143, **144**
Brady, Mathew (and assistants), photographs by, **66** (top left), **70**, **90–91**, **112** (top), **124–125** (all but Halleck), **126** (top)
Breckinridge, John C., 78
Brooks, Noah, 64
Brown, John, 77
Buchanan, James, 68, 81, 89, 91
Buena Vista, Battle of, 49, 50
Bull Run, First Battle of, 102, **102**, 103, 107,
Burnside, Ambrose E., 123, **124**
Cabinet, *See* Lincoln
Calhoun, John, 32, 54
California, admission to Union, 51, 56
Cameron, Simon, 76, 79, 111
Carondelet, 118
Cartoons, **51**, **69**, **77**, **81**, **89**, **122–123**, **130**, **139**
Cartwright, Peter, 49
Cemetery Ridge, Pa., battle at, 127
Chancellorsville, Va., battle at, 124
Charleston, S.C., 130

150

Chase, Salmon P., 76, 79, **91,** 92, 114
Chattanooga, Tenn., battle at, 130
Chickamauga, Ga., Battle of, 130
City Point, Va., 136, 138, **back endsheet**
Civil War, 95–103, 112, 114, 117–120, 123–125, 127, 128, 130, 131, 138
Clary's Grove Boys, 27, 28
Clay, Henry, 50, 53, 56, **56–57**
Cold Harbor, Va., battle at, 131
Committee of Thirteen, 81, 83
Compromise of 1850, 56, 58
Confederacy, 86, 95, 107, *See also* specific states
Congress, 112
Constitution, U.S.,
   Thirteenth Amendment to, 120, 134–135
Copperheads, 134
Cranston, L.G., painting by, **84–85**
Crawford, Andrew, 19
Crittenden, John J., 81
Crittenden Compromise, 81, 83
Cumberland, 112
Dana, Charles, 135
Davis, David, 60, 79
Davis, Jefferson, 86, 92, 94, **94,** 130
Democrats, 29, 33, 51, 54, 76, 78, 80, 130
District of Columbia,
   slave trade in, 51, 54, 56
Dorsey, Azel W., 19
Douglas, Stephen A., 41, 56, 63, 68, 69, **70,** 71, **72–73,** 74, 78, 80, 97, 98, 100
Drewry's Bluff, Va., battle at, 114
Early, Jubal, 131
Eckert, Thomas, 119
Edwards, Ninian W., 44, 47
Elections, presidential, 78–79, 82, 129, 130
Elizabethtown, Ky., 13, 14, 19
Ellsworth, Elmer E., 100
Emancipation Proclamation, 120, **121,** 123–124
England, 111, and Civil War, 107
Ericsson, John, 112
Everett, Edward, 128
Fair Oaks, Va. (Seven Pines), battle at, 116
Farragut, David, 134
Fell, Jesse W., 76
Florida, secession of, 83
Foote, Andrew, 118
Ford's Theatre, 143
Forts
   Donelson, 117
   Henry, 117
   Jefferson, 86
   Monroe, 97, 114
   Moultrie, 92
   Pickens, 86
   Sumter, 86, 92, 96, **96–97,** 97
France, and Civil War, 107
Francis, Mrs. Simeon, 44
Fredericksburg, Va., battle at, 123, 124
Frémont, John C., 64, 77, 110, 134
Fugitive Slave Law, 54, 58
Gardner, Alexander, photograph by, **143**
Gentry, Allen, 22–23
Gentry, James, 22
Gentryville, Ind., 22
Georgia, 134, secession of, 83
Gettysburg, Pa., Battle of, 118, 127, 128
Gettysburg Address, 126, **127,** 128
Gettysburg Cemetery, 126, **126,** 128
Gist, William H., 81
Graham, Mentor, 28, 32
Grant, Ulysses S., 117, 125, **125,** 127, 128, 130, 131, **132–133,** 134, **136–137,** 138, 142
Greeley, Horace, 97, 100, 138
Green, Bowling, 32, 33
Halleck, Henry W., 117, **124,** 127, 128
Halstead, Murat, 79
Hamlin, Hannibal, 82, **82**
Hampton Roads, Va., 112, 114
Hanks, Dennis, 10, 17, 18, 21, 22, **150**
Hanks, John, 24, 79, **150**
Harpers Ferry, Va., 77, 97, 98
Harrison, William Henry, 50, 53
Harrison's Landing, Va., 117
Hay, John, 100, 120, 134
Hazel, Caleb, 15
Healy, G.P.A., paintings by, **68, 136–137**
Herndon, William H., **41,** 43, 54, 59, 61–64, 68, 83, 84
Hooker, Joseph, 124, **124,** 127
Hunter, David, 114
Illinois and Michigan Canal, 35, 38, 39
Illinois State Bank, 45, 46
Ironclads, 112, **115,** 118, *See also* specific names
Island No. 10, 118
Jackson, Andrew, 38
Jackson, Stonewall, 114, **115,** 120
James River, 117
Jayne, Julia, 44
Johnson, Andrew, **129,** 134

151

Johnson, Eastman, *paintings by,* **20, 66**
Johnston, John, 10, 24
Johnston, Joseph E., 116, 131, 138, 142
Johnston, Matilda, 10
Johnston, Sarah, 10
Johnston, Sarah Bush, *See* Lincoln, Sarah Bush
Kentucky, 39, 100, 111
Knob Creek, Ky., **11,** 12, 14, 15
Lawrence, Kansas, 130
Lee, Robert E., 98, **115,** 116, 117, 119, 120, 123, 124, 127, 128, 130, 134, 138
Lincoln, Abraham, **cover, front endsheet, 4–5, 6, 9, 20, 25, 26, 28, 45, 59, 61, 68, 71, 75, 82, 87, 88, 89, 91, 103, 106, 113, 126, 129, 132–133, 135, 136–137, 140–141, 142, 143, back endsheet**
　ancestry, 12
　appeal for troops, 97, 99, 100
　assassination of, 143–145, **144**
　assassination plot against, 88, 89
　birth, 12, 15
　and border states, 116
　cabinet of, 91, 92, 111, 112, 120, 123, 134, 138
　childhood, 10
　as commander in chief, 102, 103, 107, 110, 114, 117, 124, 128
　Cooper Union address by, 76, 78
　debates with Douglas, 69–71, **72–73,** 73, 74
　descriptions of, 58, 64, 135, 138
　education, 15, 19, 21, 32, 58
　elected, to Congress, 49
　　to Illinois legislature, 28, 32
　　to Presidency, 79, 80, 134
　Emancipation Proclamation, 120, **121,** 123–124
　family life, 60, 61, 111, 124–125, 134
　fights, Jack Armstrong, 27, 28
　　Sac and Fox tribe, 28, 29
　and Fort Sumter, 92, 94, 96
　funeral of, **144,** 145
　Gettysburg Address, 126, **126,** 128
　inauguration of, 1860: 89, 92, **93**
　　1864: 136
　inventions of, **50,** 54
　lawyer, 40–43, 58, 59, 71
　　cases: Chicago and Alton Railroad, 59
　　　　Duff Armstrong, 59, 60, **61**
　　　　Illinois Central Railroad, 59
　office of, **42,** 54
　"Lost Speech" by, 64
　marries, 47, 48
　as postmaster, 31, 32, 35
　protests Mexican War, 49
　quoted, 7, 9, 16, 19, 21, 22, 28, 29, 31, 50, 61, 63, 64, 68, 69, 70–71, 74, 75, 77, 78, 80, 83, 84, 85, 88, 89, 94, 100, 110, 111, 114, 116, 119–120, 124, 128, 131, 135, 136, 138, 142
　slavery issue and, 15, 23, 38–39, 50, 54, 63, 70, 83, 110, 114, 116, 119–120, 138
Lincoln, Edward Baker (son), 49, 54, 61
Lincoln, Mary Todd (wife), 44, 47, **48,** 60, 61, 62, 84, 103, 111, **112,** 113, 125, **132–133,** 138, 142, 143, 145
Lincoln, Nancy Hanks (mother), 14, 18, 21
Lincoln, Robert Todd (son), 49, 61, 78, **112,** 113, 125, 138, 145
Lincoln, Samuel, 12
Lincoln, Sarah (sister), 10, 14, 18
Lincoln, Sarah Bush (stepmother), 10, 12, **15,** 29, 83
Lincoln, Tad (son), 60, 61, 62, 100, 111, **112,** 113, 124, 125, 145
Lincoln, Thomas (brother), 15, 18
Lincoln, Thomas (father), 10, 12–14, 18, 21
Lincoln, Willie (son), 60, 61, 62, 100, 111, 113, **113,** 125, 145
Lincoln family,
　hardship and illness, 15, 24
　Western migration of, **12–13,** 15, 24
Little Pigeon Creek, Ind., 10, 14, 19
Littlefield, John H., 59
Logan, Stephen T., 29, **41,** 42
Louisiana, secession of, 83
Lovejoy, Elijah P., 40
Manassas Junction, Va., battles at, 102, 120
Marye's Heights, Va., battle at, 123
McClellan, George B., **106,** 107, 108, 109, **109,** 111, 114, 116–118, 120, 123, 130, 134
McDowell, Irvin, 102, 103, 114
McLean, John, 76, 79
Meade, George Gordon, **124,** 127, 128
Medill, Joseph, 76
Merrimac, 7, 112, 114
Mexican War, 49–51, 56, 62, 107, 109
Milksick, 18, 24
Mill Creek, Ky., 14, 15
Missionary Ridge, Tenn., battle at, 130

152

Mississippi, 117, secession of, 83
Missouri Compromise, 63, 67, 81, 83
Mobile Bay, Ala., Battle of, 134
Monitor, 7, 112
New Mexico, admission to Union, 51, 56
    Texas boundary dispute, 51, 56
New Salem, 27, 28, 29, **32–33,** 38
Nicolay, John, 100, 111
Nolin Creek, Ky., **front endsheet,** 14
North Carolina, 138, secession of, 100
Offut, Denton, 24, 27
Petersburg, Va., 131, 134, 138
Pickett, George, 128
Pierce, Franklin, 63
Pioneers, **14,** 15, **16–17**
Polk, James K., 41, 49
Pope, John, 118, 119, 120
Porter, David, **136–137,** 138, **140–141**
Quantrill, William Clarke, 130
Republicans, 64, 74, 76–80, 109, 129–131, 134
Richmond, Va., 102, 114, 117, 123, 127, 138, 142
Riney, Zachariah, 15
Rollins, James S., 135
Rosecrans, William Starke, 130
Rutledge, Anne, 35
Sac and Fox tribe, 28
Sangamo Journal, 28, 40, 44, 46
Sangamon River, 24, **26,** 33
Savannah, Ga., 134
Scott, Dred, **66**
    Supreme Court Case, 68, 76
Scott, Winfield, 62, 63, 102, 103, **108,** 109, 131, **132–133**
Seven Days' Battles, 117
Seward, William H., 76, 79, 81, 89, **91,** 92, 120
Sheridan, Philip H., 131
Sherman, William Tecumseh, 117, 131, 134, **136–137,** 138, 142
Shields, James, 44, 46, 47
Shiloh, Tenn. (Pittsburg Landing), battle at, 117
Singsong party, 53, *See also* Whigs
Slavery, 15, 23, 38, 50, 51, 81
    Compromise of 1850 and, 56, 58
    Constitution, U.S. and, 120
    Crittenden Compromise and, 81, 83
    Emancipation Proclamation, 120, 123–124
    Fugitive Slave Law, 54, 58
    Kansas-Nebraska Act, 63, 64

Missouri Compromise and, 63, 81, 83
    in North, 39, 51
    in South, 38, 51, 110, 114
    Wilmot Proviso and, 50, 51, 56
South Carolina, secession of, 83, 94, 95
Sparrow, Elizabeth, 17, 18
Sparrow, Thomas, 17, 18
Speed, Joshua, 40, 63
Spencer County, Ind., 18, 24
Spotsylvania, Va., battle at, 131
Springfield, Ill., 24, 29, 38, 40, **42, 43,** 44, 54, 78, 80, 83, 145
Stanton, Edwin McMasters, 7, **91,** 111, 112, 145
Stone, Dan, 39
Stout, Elihu, **25**
Stuart, John Todd, 33, 35, 38, 40, 41, **41**
Taney, Roger, **66,** 68, 92
Taylor, Zachary, 49, 50, 53, 56, 63
Tennessee, 39, 107, 117, 118, secession of, 100
Texas, boundary dispute, 51, 56
    secession of, 83
Thirteenth Amendment, *See* Constitution
Todd, Mary, *See* Lincoln, Mary Todd
Trumbull, Lyman, 78
Union Conscription Act, 128
Union Navy Yard, 98
Union Party, *See* Republicans
Utah, admission to Union, 56
Van Buren, Martin, 38
Vandalia, Ill., 35, 38, **40**
Vicksburg, Miss., Battle of, 125, 127, 128
Villard, Henry, 74
Virginia, 107, secession of, 98
Wade, Ben, 110
Walker Amendment, *See* Fugitive Slave Law
Washburne, Elihu, **87**
Washington, D.C., 103, 108, 114, 131, *See also* District of Columbia
Washington, George, **6,** 131
Webster, Daniel, 51, 56
Welles, Gideon, 119, 128, 142
Whigs, 29, 33, 38, 49, 50, 51, 53, 54, 62, 64, 78
White House, **4–5, 84,** 116, 125, 131, 135, 138, 145
Williamsburg, Va., battle at, 114
Wilmot, David, 50, 51
Wilmot Proviso, 51, 56
Yates, Richard, 63
Zouaves, 100, 103, **104–105**

153